Lean Six Sig
Lessons from the Gemba
(Volume 1)

Brion Hurley

Contents

Introduction

As a follow-up to my first book, "Lean Six Sigma for Good," I knew that the book would not be sufficient to get most readers to engage with local nonprofits. I felt that case studies and lessons learned from those who have worked with nonprofits would be the next logical step. This book is intended to help you get closer to volunteering your skills for a worthy cause, or perhaps you could share this book with someone else to get them to volunteer.

I have reached out to numerous practitioners that have done this work, and asked them to write a chapter about their experiences, both good and bad. The proceeds of the book will be donated to the nonprofit of their choice, split evenly among the authors at the time of release.

We will be releasing the book with updates after each chapter is written, and you will receive the new chapters at no additional cost, so purchase early to get the best deal. If you know someone who would like to contribute, please have them contact me.

If you have questions for any of the authors, their contact information is provided within their chapter.

If you would like more examples of Lean and Six Sigma applied to nonprofits, or would like to download my first book for free, please visit http://LeanSixSigmaforGood.com

Thank you for reading and supporting the nonprofits of the authors!

Brion Hurley is a Lean Six Sigma Master Black Belt at Business Performance Improvement in Portland, Oregon. You can read his nonprofit example in Chapter 5.

Joe Hnat: Can a Corporate Employee Garden Feed the Hungry?

My beginnings started in Pennsylvania, in a small town called Coaldale. I found myself following around my parents, who were avid volunteers, supporting young folks like myself and the community. They were not getting paid, they didn't complain, they just did. They were "giving back" as that term is used commonly now in a world that really does need it more than ever. I decided to follow in their footsteps.

I was fortunate to attend college and enroll in a 3-2 program (3 years to complete B.A. in Physics/Engineering, and then 2 years to complete B.S. in Mechanical Engineering). Sweet deal!

I moved from Pennsylvania to Ohio to land a full-time job. Eventually, I relocated to Florida.

I've worked several "individual contributor" and manager roles. Early in my career, I was introduced to Lean. Primary Lean techniques included Value Stream Mapping (VSM), 5S, Standard Work and Visual Control. This provided a great basis for my career of over 23 years, and continues to give me that "Case for Change," a term many of you are familiar with.

THE IDEA

One day, I had an idea of starting a garden on our corporate land. I was just getting started with gardening in Florida, and it was much different than up north. If I could get a club started, the tips and tricks would be abundant, and my home garden would also start to flourish.

We had 1500 employees in the facility, and I was certain I could get some of my peers to volunteer to support this idea. I proposed it to the Facilities Manager and was denied. I didn't really have a business case. Shoot, was our company going to make profit from this idea? It could actually cost the Facility more money for having a garden on campus. It really was a setback.

I later traveled to our headquarters and picked up the local newspaper. I didn't think much of it, but found an article where someone at our headquarters was planning to start a garden on corporate land. Bingo! I got lucky.

I took the newspaper article to our Facilities Manager, and threw it down on his desk. I said, "When can we get started?"

LEAN TIP: Be persistent with your ideas, or just be lucky.

Initial Garden Space

LAUNCHING A TEAM

I formed a team, and brought everyone together for a meeting. I wanted to get alignment before we start digging. What's our mission? What do we want to produce? How would we produce the garden? What's the water source? What vegetables? The list of questions goes on.

The team responded to the questions and also agreed on volunteer times and days. The seeds were planted for making this idea into a reality!

LEAN TIP: Preparing for this meeting was very important; don't just call a meeting and hope everything is going to come together. Spend time thinking about the possible outcomes and decisions to be made.

One key finding during that meeting was determining who will be our customer. It was decided that our customer would be a local nonprofit, Daily Bread, that provides a daily meal to the hungry and homeless. Wow, fresh vegetables to folks who don't have much. Over 50% of the people that go for the meals are homeless. They live in the woods, under bridges, in cars, etc. It is a very difficult life. Knowing the customer really helps the team of volunteers get inspired to do their best.

Recipients of Daily Bread

Our team did not have a budget initially, and had to approach this with a low-cost mindset. We brainstormed ideas, and started by checking our warehouse for wood or crates that could be used for the planter boxes. We hit the jackpot early, as there were many opportunities that could be adapted for our garden.

LEAN TIP: What's that saying, "One man's trash is another man's treasure?" Check what items are being sent to the landfill before purchasing. You would be amazed what could be reused.

Warehouse planter box with young pineapple

We did need additional budget, and found out that our corporation was offering a green grant to nonprofits who were going to implement an environmental project. This was perfect!

We completed the application with the support of the nonprofit. It involved listing our goals, our project schedule, and requested budget. The application was accepted, and we got the necessary budget. Finding money or raising funds is not easy. This was another key step in getting closer to our mission.

With the planter boxes and budget, we were ready to design a layout and set up the garden. The initial plan was to have the garden within the campus. We settled on a location, but there were two major problems.

- (1) It would get heavy sun in the afternoon as it faced primarily to the west.
- (2) There was a reclaimed water sprinkler system.

These problems were not very good for beginning gardeners. We learned that it is preferred to have the garden face the east and get sun in the morning. In addition, the reclaimed water required a ton of vegetable cleaning when harvesting.

We did have some planter boxes in place with dirt. We knew this wasn't going to work, and proposed a new location. We also explained the importance of not having the reclaimed water sprayed on the garden. The Facility Manager agreed and we found a new location facing east and shaded from the west. We also got a bonus from Facilities as they agreed to install a fence around the garden. This prevented spraying onto the plants, in addition to modifying the nearby sprinklers.

LEAN TIP: Involve others in solving problems. Even though Facilities was against the garden idea initially, we brought them into our garden set up. We explained the reclaimed water issue, and they offered the fence. That was much easier than asking for a fence.

The garden area was 20' x 40' and included 6 planter boxes, a water source, and lots of soil to be added. We started small, as there was plenty of room for more planters. We wanted to prove the concept first and then expand. You can apply the principle of starting small and testing your hypothesis to multiple things in life.

Corporate garden

Nonprofit Garden

YEAR 1

First year was a year of learning. We had lots of ideas and inputs. The energy was great, but it was not directed and ended up being a "free for all" for planting several different types of vegetables. Seeds and seedlings were plenty, and it didn't matter if it was the right season for it. We had all kinds of vegetables; tomatoes, cucumbers, onions, squash, eggplants, broccoli, carrots, and watermelons.

Plethora of Vegetables

The "fun" experiment stopped when the watermelon basically took over the garden. Watermelon (if you don't know) tends to send out long branches in every direction. It started to mask several planter boxes. It was time to shut it down and remove the watermelon. I call this the GWP – "Great Watermelon Pause".

We weren't gardeners from education or upbringing, but we did have a mission to feed those who are hungry and homeless, and we needed to figure this out. We did some homework and came up with new plans for the next planting season.

LEAN TIP: Take additional time for your initial project plans. Don't be tempted to use up your energy no matter what. Get smart before diving in!

YEAR 2

The second season had much more success. The team came together, studied the type of plants for the season, and limited the type of plants. We even met with our customer (the chef at the nonprofit) and determined that their need was salad specific vegetables. Understanding customer requirements is underestimated at times.

LEAN TIP: A simple "ask" of your customer will yield very positive results.

YEAR 3

For the following 3 years, the recipe of limiting the number of vegetables and planting at the right time yielded a large amount of vegetables. It was amazing! Unfortunately, we didn't measure our success by number of bags or number of pounds. It was more about just dropping off vegetables, knowing that they were going to a very good cause.

The nonprofit is open 365 days each year. Our team volunteered at the gardens on a routine basis, mainly meeting on the weekends. A few volunteers found it easier to work right after work. Either way, when it was time to harvest the vegetables, it was a 5 minute drive to the nonprofit to drop off the vegetables at their food distribution warehouse. From there, the food would be transported to the kitchen, and the chefs would use the fresh vegetables in their daily meals.

LEAN TIP: Transportation time (one of the 8 forms of waste) should not be underestimated. A quick commute to drop off vegetables was simple and easy. We did implement a garden right next to the Food Distribution Warehouse, and the commute is less than 30 seconds walking. That's even better!

Over the years, the garden has served as a way to educate many of the volunteers, along with the visitors. Connecting with a local Girl

Scout troop was an excellent way for our team to share gardening tips, and also get some good muscle in helping remove weeds. As you lead or participate in Lean Projects, consider different paths that have intangible benefits. I didn't realize how much fun and how appreciative it would be to provide a few garden tips. Hopefully this outreach sparked one of the young girls into doing the same for other generations.

Girl Scouts volunteers at the corporate garden

YEAR 4

In year four, I wanted to expand the corporate gardening by soliciting other corporations in the area, to see if they would start a garden on their land. A presentation package was created that included the proposal, benefits, necessary resources, lessons learned and estimated time frame. It was a simple package, but had a good recipe for any corporation to start a garden. I sent out the package to five local companies. It wasn't a slam dunk. However, I actually had one company take it seriously. Eventually, in year five, they received grant money through their corporate headquarters, and will start a garden in the fall. It's a start, and I think there will be other local companies that will follow.

LEAN TIP: Your initial proposal will always need a revision. I made 5 or so revisions to the corporate package. Be open to feedback, and then be brave in sending it out.

Volunteering is contagious, and is the heart of any nonprofit. I have volunteered with many good folks over the years. I was always impressed on how each person gave up their personal time, and didn't ask for anything in return. Though, as you might already know, volunteering has such good internal rewards.

After our volunteers witness where the vegetables go, they get such a great feeling inside. Each person knows they are making a difference in someone's life, and they are humbled in knowing what they have.

Corporate Volunteers

LESSONS LEARNED

One technique that has been helpful is capturing lessons learned. I used this technique extensively during Lean workshops. At the end of the event, I would take 10-15 minutes, and just listen to the input from team members (I called it the "good, bad and ugly").

As a Lean Facilitator, this was tremendous feedback, and allowed me to improve our Lean workshops fairly quickly.

During one stint in my career, we held an event every 2 weeks for an entire year, as part of a major lean transformation in our facility!

Over the past 5 years, I would capture lessons learned from our garden volunteers, and this again would prove to be a valuable tool in helping us better the garden. I'll share a few of the key takeaways:

- **Lesson #1: Your initial adversary might be your biggest advocate**

As I mentioned earlier, Facilities rejected my first proposal with the garden. As time went on, Facilities has become a great supporter. They installed a fence around the garden, provided materials, supported trash removal, and even boast about the garden. Facilities even allowed us to add a nature trail on campus that leads to a gazebo, surrounded by native plants to attract local butterflies. They started to install native plants at entrance ways, rather than annuals (that just die and need to be replaced). Even though we didn't hit it off at first, they have become a long-term partner in making the garden what it is today.

In my factory days, I found this to be true as well. Once I was able to convince a person on the use of Lean tools and methods, that person typically became a big supporter and user of the tools.

- **Lesson #2: Having volunteers to support the garden has not been easy**

I figured I could get 5% of the employee population (5% of 1500 = 75). Then I thought I could get 4%...then 3%...or maybe 2%? We ended up with 30 or so folks on a garden email distribution (about 2%).

As for regular volunteers, it has been about 2-5 people. The tough part is getting folks to take that initial step to join in the activities. I have asked, begged, and tried several different ways to get folks to volunteer. There are the occasional taste testing that occurs (you do need to make sure the veggies taste good before you deliver them).

Then, there's a t-shirt that is provided after someone volunteers a few times. We have an internal webpage where postings are made showing pictures of the vegetables and volunteers.

Social media is popular, so this technique is driving some participation. I'm still learning on this lesson as you can tell.

One day, we will have 20 regular volunteers, and our garden production will be "off the charts!"

- **Lesson #3: Gardening for fun could lead to serious gardening**

I'm addicted, just ask my wife. If she is looking for me, I'm either at the nonprofit gardens, or out in the yard. I've read several books and articles, watched tons of YouTube videos, talked to local experts, listened to the employees who have been gardening for years, etc. I'm still learning as one of my latest topics is "Food Foresting" (Google it!).

If there was a MBA in Gardening, I would sign up. There is so much to learn about gardening from the soil preparation, types of water sources (my favorite is a rain barrel, ask me about our guide to make your own), various vegetables, compost methods, harvest plans, etc. I don't consider myself an expert, I'm just a regular guy having fun at something he really enjoys.

- **Lesson #4: Producing vegetables will have its success and failures**

I still recall the first year where we sprouted so many types of vegetables. It was fun, but wasn't a good year for production. We might have gotten a few of every type. In the end, the nonprofit really couldn't do much with that. Also, there have been those days where the pests come out of nowhere. We had success one year with broccoli. The heads were much larger than what you see in the store, and the taste was great. I even learned that once you remove the first head, the plant will produce 3-4 baby heads. I thought the plant only produced one time and then you removed it. Ok, enough with this small lesson on broccoli.

The second year was different. As the plants started to grow, a pest takeover commenced, and ate up the entire patch. It was tough to see, and it was a gentle reminder on pest control. At our garden, we don't use chemical pesticides. So, it is more of a "observe and pick," meaning pick off the worms or critters that are doing damage to the vegetables. There's so much to say on this subject and I will give you one tip. Buy ladybugs and release them in your garden. You'll be surprised how well they fend off the bad insects, and provide tons of enjoyment to your children when they find a ladybug on the tip of their finger.

- **Lesson #5: The endless smiles from volunteers doesn't get old**

No further comments on this lesson.

Diversity of Volunteers

Well, I hope you enjoyed my little journey in gardening and supporting a nonprofit. It is similar to the Lean journey I do in my professional career; same tools/techniques, similar motivational discussions, similar performance tracking, and similar lessons learned.

I will encourage you to participate in your local community and find a nonprofit that you can support.

Find out your passion by just jumping in! It will take time and dedication, but you will find an unbelievable internal reward.

Author in orange shirt with Gang of Gardeners

I personally found that gardening was my passion, and the reward was giving to those who are in need.

If you answered "yes" to my story's title, and would like more information about starting a corporate garden, please email or connect with me below. Thanks!

About the Author, Joe Hnat III

From small town to large corporation, I've been volunteering for 20+ years from coaching sports, building houses, mentoring folks and supporting nonprofits. I have a background in Mechanical Engineering from Pennsylvania State University, and continue to problem solve in my corporate world and extracurricular activities. I am married to a lovely lady who keeps me healthy with diet and yoga, and have one child who continues to amaze me with her talents of art and music. I am fortunate and know that what I do helps other people. I hope my story inspires you to find a local non-profit and support them with the best skills you have. Thanks. Now, go dig!

Email: jhinmb@gmail.com

LinkedIn: https://www.linkedin.com/in/joseph-hnat-iii-a1469878/

About the Nonprofit, Daily Bread

Daily Bread, Inc. ensures that no one in Brevard County faces hunger or homelessness alone. We have empowered, supported and assisted those confronting financial challenges to become self-sufficient. We do not provide a "hand-out", rather we offer a "hand-up." Feeding the hungry and the homeless is an important part of what we do, but is not all that we do. We help individuals – through a comprehensive array of programs and services – navigate their way to self-sufficiency.

Location: Melbourne, Florida, USA

Website: http://dailybreadinc.org/

The author has asked that 100% of his proceeds from the book will go to Daily Bread.

Pat O'Connor: Lessons from a Flag Program and Ushering

Revision Number: v1
Original Issue Date: 08/03/2018

I'm Pat O'Connor. I've been a Lean Six Sigma (LSS) Black Belt (BB) for the last 12 years. I've done volunteer work in various capacities for many years. First I'll briefly share the most significant volunteer work with which I'm currently involved. Then I'll share lessons I've learned while doing volunteer work. Some of the lessons are related to how I've leveraged my LSS skills, some aren't particularly related to LSS skills but you may still find them helpful. You can contact me at pjseco@yahoo.com.

Chair, Avenue of the Flags Program

The Avenue of the Flags Program is a community pride and fundraising program run by volunteers. On the 5 Flag Holidays (Memorial Day, Flag Day, Independence Day, Labor Day, and Veterans Day) flags are set out at dawn and taken down at dusk at subscribers' homes and businesses. It is a beautiful display of patriotism, and funds go to youth organizations.

The volunteers that run the program are from my local chapter of The Optimists. Optimist International is a worldwide volunteer organization made up of more than 2,500 local clubs whose members work each day to make the future brighter by bringing out the best in children, their communities, and themselves. Our motto is Friend of Youth.

The Flags Program was conceived by an Optimist club in Iowa. Several other clubs in Iowa, including mine, soon adopted it, and it has spread to other clubs from there. I was not an Optimist member when the Program was conceived; nor was I an Optimist member when my club adopted the Program. When I joined my club I became involved as a volunteer in our Program, and then after a few years I became our Chair.

The Flags Program is essentially a small business. There are customers, sales people, customer database managers, invoicing, flag assemblers, sleeve installers, flag setters, and external workers (flag setters that are not club members).

When I got involved I quickly became invested in the Program. At that time we were setting several hundred flags each Flag Holiday. The processes worked but I saw opportunity to improve our effectiveness and efficiency, and I saw a need to assess and mitigate risk; I felt doing such would be necessary if we wanted to continue to expand. And thanks to the efforts of our great members we have definitely expanded. When asked if I was interested in being the Chair, I felt I was called to it. It has been my honor to be the Chair. My LSS skills have really helped me in my role as Chair. We are now setting over eleven hundred flags every Flag Holiday. There is an evident community pride amongst our subscribers, and we bring in over $44,000 a year for youth programs in our community.

Head Usher

My Church has over one thousand parishioners, 3 Masses a week, and about 60 ushers. I have been an usher in my Church for years. When the head usher position came open and I was asked whether I would take the position I agreed right away. I believed that it was my time, that my LSS experience could bring value, and that it would be good for me.

Usher duties include greeting parishioners, helping parishioners find seats, taking up the collection, identifying parishioners that receive Communion from their pews (i.e. that find it difficult go to the front of the Church for Communion), handing out bulletins, and doing a quick cleanup of the Church after Mass.

Sustainability Squad Steering Team Member

The Sustainability Squad is an Employee Resource Group (ERG) at my place of work. It is a voluntary organization of employees that work toward:

- Minimizing our company's and employee's impact on the plant
- Improving health, wellbeing, and quality of life.

While I am drawn to sustainability to an appreciable degree, when this ERG was established my primary reason for joining was that I felt my LSS skills were needed given how well LSS aligns with sustainability.

Other

I have volunteered in other capacities, such as coaching youth sports, and one day events to improve my community.

I've taught numerous LSS classes, through which I've gained relevant lessons learned.

Lessons Learned

Process documentation – process maps

One of the first things I did when I became Chair of the Flags program was to sit with someone who knew the program well and map the processes. Initially I thought there was one process. However, the act of mapping helped me realize there were multiple processes. Ultimately we captured the program in five swim lane process maps and created a sixth map that showed at a high level how the five maps related. There are more than five processes, but after doing those five I was getting enough understanding of the program that we decided to leave it at that. Below are two of the process maps. Note that the maps are shared as high level examples; it is not the intent to share the details of the process steps.

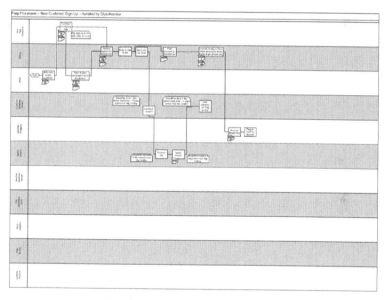

Flag process for New Customer Sign Up

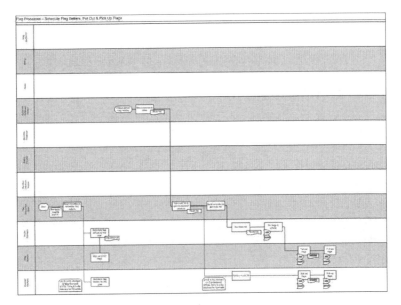

Flag Setter process

Creating the process maps

- Raised my understanding of the program as a whole, which made me a better Chair. I had been doing some roles in the process (flag setter, route captain) but I wasn't very familiar with the other roles.
- Laid a foundation for the key players in the process to understand roles beyond their own.
- Made transition of work easier.
- Helped upstreams understand their impact on downstreams.
- Highlighted that there are multiple domains to the work. You get a feel for the domains by noticing how the work is separated by groups of swim lanes in the maps above.

  * The physical (assembling, storing, maintaining, setting and picking up flags, installing sleeves), and the logical (collecting and maintaining customer information, defining the boundaries of routes, defining who is responsible for which routes) domains.

* The customer facing (sales, invoicing, installing sleeves, flag setting, trouble handling), external worker facing (recruiting, communicating, directing), and back office (information management) domains.

Process mapping MADE THINGS VISIBLE. In my LSS experience I have found the principle of making things visible, when applicable, to be very high leverage. Of course, as always, use the tools warranted but don't create waste by using tools that are not warranted. I have not done swim lane process mapping on my other volunteering efforts because I didn't see that there would be the benefit for the effort.

Process mapping led to job shadowing, discussed below.

Process documentation – standard operating procedures (SOPs) and layouts

- SOPs are useful. As head usher I documented the usher duties for a basic Mass, and for roughly a dozen special cases such as when there is a baptism during Mass, taking annual head count during Mass, Ash Wednesday, etc. The SOPs for the special cases have highlighted the deltas from the basic Mass. See below

Standard Operating Procedures for Basic Mass and Head Count

- For Easter and Christmas we hold Masses in the gym. It was helpful to have a document that shows the layout of the gym. It makes visible the flow of how collection baskets will be passed and how people will go up to receive Communion.

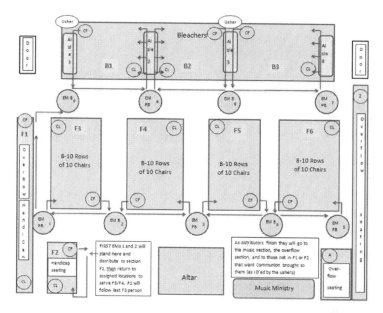

Gym layout for Easter and Christmas Mass

Walk the process / job shadow

As mentioned above, process mapping led to job shadowing. I recommend job shadowing for all the key players in your processes, especially those in leadership positions.

After process mapping the Flags program I job shadowed the customer database manager, the Treasurer, invoicing, and several flag setter groups including an external worker group. Although I had been a flag setter, I had set just my routes – job shadowing other flag setters gave me insight into things I didn't learn from doing my own route. Job shadowing gave me a much better appreciation of the whole, strengthened relationships, and made me a better Chair.

Whenever we have new ushers, we have them job shadow twice before being put on the list of ushers. One time they job shadow an usher working one of the sides of the Church, and one time they job shadow an usher working the middle of the Church. We do it this way because there are some different responsibilities for the sides versus the middle.

Understand what is Critical To (CT) satisfaction / listen

When I became head usher, I asked a cross section of my ushers to be on a temporary committee so I could listen to their improvement ideas for our ministry, and then we implemented the ideas. I also listened to what our Priest wanted from the ushers and implemented his ideas. This yielded several dozen improvement ideas including instituting a lost and found, instituting a process for capturing suggestions from parishioners, adding quick references to the usher room for things like dealing with blood borne pathogens, adding signs around the Church that direct toward the handicap bathroom, replacing baby changing tables with wall mounted Koala style fold out baby changing stations to free up space in the restrooms, etc. I highly recommend listening to understand CTs and implementing value add ideas.

Over time in my role as Chair of the Flags program I came to understand what was important to my Flag committee members, and thus came to understand "paying those that work for free". Endeavor to understand how your volunteers get "paid". You can gain this understanding by listening and observing, or asking directly. Ways volunteers get paid include:

- By doing good, i.e. helping the organization realize its goals.
- The fulfillment of using their skills
- The fulfillment of seeing thru commitments they have made
- By being needed and valued
- By honing leadership skills
- The social interaction afforded by being part of a team

Although this isn't a hard and fast rule, I've noticed that the payments can have some alignment with a volunteers age/stage in life, personality traits, etc. For example, payments may align with whether the volunteer is:

- Still in school, just joined the work world, has been in the work world many years, is retired.
- Single, married, married with children, empty nest.
- Introverted or extroverted.
- Has good people skills, has good technical skills.

One volunteer may be fully booked with work, spouse, children, etc. Another may be retired and have an empty nest. The first may see social interactions at meetings as a waste of scarce time, while the other sees it as a primary reason for being a volunteer. I suggest being sensitive to these CTs. Consider whether the busy person is needed in person for any/all of a meeting – perhaps they can send their status by email and not attend, or be first on the agenda and leave early. This way you can respect their time and not take away the socialization that others value.

5S

We did a 5S in the usher room at my Church. It went well, and the gains have been pretty well sustained.

- The thing I liked best about it was the use of labels with text and pictures. For example, we designated space on a shelf for a set of collection baskets. So we put a label on the section of the shelf where the baskets were to be kept, and the label has the words "collection baskets" and a picture of that set of collection baskets (there are several different styles/sizes of collection baskets) in the usher room.

I led a 5S of a storage room in the basement of the Church. It was in disarray and over a dozen groups (Marriage Encounter, Boy Scouts, janitorial, etc) had things in the room. I learned a few lessons from this experience.

- I assumed (through my experience at work) that if I scheduled a meeting, then most/all of the invitees would take it as an obligation to attend and therefore would come. This was not the case. Without realizing it at the time, I was taking for granted that all of these volunteers had the meeting attendance etiquette of employees in my company. I should have been more diligent in impressing upon them that they needed to attend, and that they would directly benefit from attending by getting an organized, sustainable storage room from their involvement.
- There was good attendance at the Sort meeting, at which we did Sort (including red tags), but after the red tag time frame expired we had only me and one other person at the Set meeting.
- My interpretation is that people wanted to ensure their stuff didn't get sorted out so they came to the Sort meeting. But they didn't come to the Set meeting because they didn't really care where it was set, and they didn't appreciate that doing a good Set, Shine, and Standardize improves your chances of sustaining the gains. I should have done more to impress upon them the need to come to the Set meeting, and not just assume they would come because they were invited.
- I and the other person did the Set, Shine, and Standardize. The room was in good order when we were done. Predictably the room has lost some of its organization over time, but it has retained much of the benefit of the 5S. When I occasionally check in on it, I see that it isn't maintained at its entitlement state. I've asked a few people that use the room for their level of satisfaction and they are pretty pleased with it. So there is a lesson learned, the standard/satisfaction of the Belt/facilitator

(me) isn't as important as the standard/satisfaction of the customers (i.e. users of the room).

Suggestion Program

As mentioned above, at my Church we instituted a suggestion capture and resolution process that runs thru the ushers. It gives parishioners an avenue for getting issues resolved quickly, and it frees up the Priests to focus on Mass and the congregation rather than addressing issues. Over 100 issues (some are recurring like reloading hand towels and toilet paper, or doing light maintenance like tightening a loose screw in a kneeler) have been handled in about 3 years. I believe this has been significant to parishioner and Priest satisfaction. I recommend assessing whether a suggestion capture and resolution process makes sense for your work.

General Advice

Here is general advice that others have told me that I've found to be true:

- As you are thinking about doing your work, think about how you can do your work better.
- 5S and standard work bring order. Order breeds quality and quality breeds order. It is easier to make improvements that are sustainable when work is standardized and things are orderly.
- Cadence, such as having periodic meetings and sending informational emails, is important.

* In the Flags program we have prep meetings as our busy times (invoicing, the first Flag Holiday) approach.
* At my Church we have an annual refresher meeting for all

ministries, and I periodically send emails to my ushers to let them know what is being discussed at the monthly Liturgical Ministers meetings.

Proceeds

Any proceeds attributed to my chapter will be donated to the Catherine McAuley Center. A number of years ago I was a volunteer there helping a young man new to this country improve his English. That was my only volunteer experience there, and I didn't use any LSS, but a connection was made. Although I no longer give time to the Catherine McAuley Center, I do support them financially. Learn more about them at http://CatherineMcAuleyCenter.org

Andrew Parris: International Relief and Development Improvement

My educational and professional background

I am a certified Lean Six Sigma (LSS) Master Black Belt with a B.S. in Manufacturing in Engineering from University of California Berkeley, and an M.S. in Technology & Policy and a PhD in Mechanical Engineering from the Massachusetts Institute of Technology (MIT). I earned my PhD as part of the "Lean Aircraft Initiative," an MIT research consortium tasked with assessing if and how Lean applies to the design and production of aircraft. After UC Berkeley and before MIT, I worked for 3Com in Silicon Valley as a Manufacturing Engineer on their assembly line making Ethernet adapter cards. After MIT and the following year in the Gordon–Conwell Theological Seminary, I worked for 11 years for Lockheed Martin (LM), mostly in process improvement on the Atlas Rocket Program. There I grew in my understanding and application of LSS. LM had a large and fruitful "LM21 Operating Excellence" initiative, through which I got trained as a Six Sigma Black Belt and a LSS Master Black Belt. In this time, I facilitated over 20 process improvement projects and taught LSS thinking and tools to many Green Belts and leaders.

How I transitioned to working for an NGO, and what I found there

I left Lockheed Martin to work for World Vision International[1], a large Christian, nongovernmental organization (NGO). Active in about 80 countries, World Vision undertakes transformational development to help communities escape poverty and provides emergency relief to people affected by crisis or disaster.

The book Walking with the Poor[2] inspired me to make this change. In this book, the author Bryant Meyers, a former World Vision senior leader, explains transformational development – World Vision's approach to helping communities out of poverty. The basic idea is that World Vision "development facilitators" don't come into a poor village and tell people what to do, or, worse yet, do things for them. Instead, the development facilitator (DF) helps the community to dream of a better future and what changes they would like to see. Then the DF works with them to identify the causes of poverty and to develop interventions that will help move the community out of poverty. The DF builds up the capacity of the community along the way, and teaches them what they need to know and do to improve their lives, and to sustain the gains long after World Vision has left. Ideally, the community helps to create and owns the plans and the projects that are undertaken. They also provide their expertise and at least some of the resources to do the work. Together, the community and the DF work, learn and grow as they transform the community out of poverty and into a sustainable path of development in pursuit of "life in all its fullness" for all members of the community, and especially the most vulnerable.

As I read Walking with the Poor, I was struck by the similarity between the role of World Vision's development facilitator and my role in Lockheed Martin as a process improvement facilitator. I was not coming in, analyzing processes, and telling people what to do.

---

[1]https://www.wvi.org/
[2]https://amzn.to/2igBb1s

Rather, I was training and coaching the people performing a process to see the waste in it, to analyze it, to identify root causes, and to develop and experiment with countermeasures. Like a DF, I was working with people to help them create, own and implement plans to sustainably improve how they performed their work. The kinship I felt with the DF made me want to join World Vision, and a year later I did.

The highlight of my time with World Vision was three years that I lived in Nairobi, Kenya, with my family while working with all nine of the World Vision East Africa Region offices. Prior to taking on that role, during a business trip I made to Uganda, Tanzania and Burundi, I gave a brief "Process Excellence" training that I had developed. The response to this training was so positive that several people told me with excitement and sincerity, "Andrew, what you are teaching us is wonderful! This is new for us. You must come here to teach and help us to do these things!" And less than a year later I did. The diagram below shows the vision of Process Excellence that I developed for World Vision. It seamlessly integrates LSS (more on the top) and transformational development principles (more on the bottom).

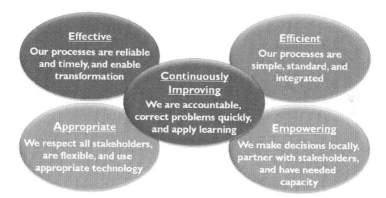

Process Excellence as I defined it – an integration of Lean Six Sigma and development principles

When I arrived in Nairobi, I found process problems similar to what one may find in any service organization or in the office processes of a manufacturing company. The difference was that the problems were generally greater in magnitude because of the weaker infrastructure, higher uncertainty, lower levels of education, and a culture that more readily accepted and lived with problems, rather than seeking to solve them. To put it in a positive light: I found many opportunities for improvement.

Even more importantly, I found many **people** who were frustrated with the inefficiencies and waste, people who were eager to learn a new way of thinking and acting, and ready to improve. In those three years in East Africa, as described further below, I trained, coached and worked with my colleagues there to achieve not only significant measurable impact, but also changes in the work culture.

Photos of World Vision's Water, Sanitation & Hygiene (WASH) work in East Africa

My transition to humanitarian NGO work, and what I found there

After nine years with World Vision, I joined Medair[3] in their headquarters office near Lausanne, Switzerland, where I am now. Medair, a smaller Christian humanitarian NGO operating in about a dozen countries, relieves suffering and brings hope to people af-

---

[3]https://www.medair.org/

fected by crises in some of the hardest to reach and most devastated places. In about a dozen countries afflicted by war and natural disasters, Medair provides humanitarian assistance primarily in the sectors of Health & Nutrition, WASH, and Shelter & Infrastructure. For example, our field staff:

- Treat children and pregnant & breastfeeding women for malnutrition in South Sudan and Somalia
- Support and/or operate health clinics in Iraq and Democratic Republic (DR) of the Congo
- Help Rohingya refugees build shelters (out of wood and tarps) in Bangladesh
- Help displaced Syrians survive inside and outside of their country

In Medair, I found the same challenges as World Vision, but even more extreme. Emergency response and recovery work is incredibly complex and challenging. Which company willingly works in the most difficult, most disastrous, hardest to reach and most unpredictable contexts? We do. Medair operates in countries in crisis such as Syria, Iraq, Afghanistan, South Sudan, and DR Congo. We work in five of the ten most corrupt countries in the world. We face overwhelming challenges of corruption, violence, unpredictability, poor infrastructure, difficult terrain, extreme weather, and inadequate resources.

Photo of damage in Indonesia after an earthquake and tsunami on 28 and 29 September 2018

Children in a remote area of Afghanistan where Medair provides community-based nutrition services at around thirty rural and urban sites

Because of these extreme contexts and the waste that these generate, I believe the humanitarian industry has the greatest need of any industry to optimize systems and minimize waste. Not only this, but because our work directly touches the lives of those who suffer almost unbearable challenges, every improvement we make can literally save lives. **Improvement in a humanitarian NGO is** not just a formal aspiration. It is a moral obligation.

The tools and techniques I used to help them

In World Vision and Medair, the first thing I did was not to apply tools and techniques myself, but to equip and inspire my colleagues to improve their work. In East Africa, I trained 370 World Vision colleagues with the one-day "Process Excellence Energiser" course I developed. This course combines hands-on experiential learning (through a three-hour simulation) with theory and tools that equip and inspire people to begin to make small changes in how they do their day-to-day work. In World Vision, I also trained nearly 50 colleagues in East Africa and another 50 in other countries as LSS Green Belts. Before I left East Africa, I organized LSS Black Belt training for a dozen of my best LSS Green Belts, so that they could lead LSS in their offices after I left.

Instructor Prashant Pal (2nd from left) and me (3rd from right) with World Vision LSS BBs

My friend Sammy Obara[4], Lean Master and a senior partner at Honsha[5], helped me find five outstanding LSS experts who developed and provided pro bono training for this group, and who also facilitated improvement workshops for World Vision. These were (in order of their visits to East Africa):

- Prashant Pal[6], a LSS MBB who at the time was leading Process Excellence in Accenture in India. He founded and is CEO of PURE India Trust[7], which empowers underprivileged people by providing education and employment through skill and entrepreneurship development.
- Anil Gupta[8], a LSS MBB who is a LSS instructor and consultant. Now with The Poirier Group[9], he helps organizations achieve strategic transformations through strategic planning and execution, and LSS capacity building.
- Toni Davies[10], a Lean sensei who is founder and CEO of Davies Consulting[11]. Toni consults, coaches and trains to bring about organizational transformation. She worked for Productivity Press in its early years and collaborated with some of the early Lean leaders, including Shigeo Shingo and Ryuji Fukuda to make their ideas and practices known worldwide.
- Sandor Bende-Farkas[12], a LSS MBB who works as a LSS trainer and consultant with ifss[13], teaching and helping organizations to solve problems.
- Christian Wolcott[14], a Lean Master and change agent, now

[4]https://www.linkedin.com/in/sammyobara/

[5]http://www.honsha.org/

[6]https://www.linkedin.com/in/prashant-pal-3488071a/

[7]https://www.pureindia.org/

[8]https://www.linkedin.com/in/anil-gupta-070b831/

[9]https://www.thepoiriergroup.com/

[10]https://www.linkedin.com/in/toni-d-706750/

[11]http://daviesconsultinginc.com/

[12]https://www.linkedin.com/in/s%C3%A1ndor-bende-farkas-2602668/

[13]https://www.ifss.net/

[14]https://www.linkedin.com/in/christian-wolcott-8b61602a/

with Optima Associates[15], focused on inspiring organizational excellence in a variety of organizations and sectors.

Sammy also organized several colleagues from Honsha to each give a webinar on Lean to the World Vision Process Excellence Community of Practice. One of these, Lean expert Ben Hoseus[16], also visited Medair twice to provide pro bono Lean support. Ben is a Lean consultant and started his own nonprofit SpreadPropserity Intl[17], which utilizes lean principles to transform humanitarian returns through insight, engagement, and investment. Ben delivered some training to my LSS Green Belts, helped plan and facilitate a creative workshop, and thoughtfully analyzed our Process Excellence initiative and provided insightful recommendations for the path forward.

---

[15]https://www.optimanow.com/
[16]https://www.linkedin.com/in/ben-hoseus/
[17]https://spreadprosperity.org/

In Medair, I gave my Process Excellence Energiser training to over 110 Medair colleagues in our headquarters in Switzerland, and to over 70 Medair field staff where we operate, and I have given two LSS Green Belt courses. The people I trained applied the thinking and tools and have achieved some important, but (due to a variety of challenges) unmeasurable results.

In both World Vision and Medair, the people I trained applied the same fundamental concepts and tools of Lean and Six Sigma that apply in private sector office processes and service operations: customer value, waste, process mapping and analysis, flow, pull, standard work, mistake-proofing, visual management, root cause problem-solving, improvement projects, facilitating Kaizen workshops, and continuous improvement in pursuit of excellence. As you can see from this list, I emphasize Lean more than Six Sigma. I do this because Lean concepts and tools are easier to learn and apply. They are also more relevant to processes with high levels of waste and variation, as is the case with most processes in developing world and crisis contexts.

While I have facilitated a few process improvement teams and meetings, my main role after training has been to encourage and coach my trainees in World Vision and Medair as they apply the LSS thinking and tools in their work and with their colleagues.

The results we achieved

The most significant documented improvements came during the three years I was committed 100% to leading process improvement in the World Vision East Africa Region. The following table showcases some of our improvements. It is taken from my article "Improving Processes for Good in East Africa[18]," which more fully documents this experience.

Country	Process	Measure	Before	After	Change
Burundi	Procurement planning and sourcing	Annual cost of goods (mosquito nets, office supplies, vehicles...)	$458,713	$318,823	-30%
Ethiopia	Recruitment	Time to hire new staff	130 days	41 days	-68%
Kenya	Procurement	Time to procure and drill boreholes	174 days	64 days	-63%
Rwanda	Procurement	Internal time to procure goods	27 days	14 days	-48%
South Sudan	Payroll	Time to prepare payroll	30 days	8 days	-73%
South Sudan	Travel and lodging	Expenses per month (January-April)	$88,683	$63,680	-28%
Uganda	Payment	Percent of documents with errors	40%	4%	-90%

In addition to these quantifiable results, all the training and many smaller improvements contributed to a change in culture. My

---

[18]"Improving Processes for Good in East Africa", © Emerald Group Publishing Limited, published in The TQM Journal 29 August 2013, Vol. 25, No. 5, pp. 458-472.

World Vision colleagues became more focused on providing customer value, they knew what waste was and tried to reduce it, and they applied a variety of Lean practices to their work, such as standard work, visual management and mistake-proofing.

In Medair, it has been much more difficult to document quantitative improvements in our processes. Several factors have contributed to this:
• the unpredictability and significant variation in our work together with relatively high employee turnover (people change roles or leave the organization before they complete their process improvement project)
• people are over-stretched (and thus have no time for data collection), and
• my own assignment to other responsibilities (that has reduced the time I could spend on training, facilitating and coaching process improvement).

Still, we have completed a handful of improvement projects, and the colleagues I trained have documented over 50 smaller "Make it Better" improvements. As well, the training and improvements are impacting our culture in good ways. Here are some examples:
• We mapped, analyzed and simplified the proposal development process – how we create proposals to institutional donors such as the United States Office of Foreign Development Assistance (OFDA) or the European Commission's Humanitarian Aid and Civil Protection Department (ECHO). We identified bottlenecks and other sources of waste, analyzed root causes of some problems, and developed a simpler and less wasteful standard process.
• A handful of teams have started to hold daily stand-up meetings to improve communication, collaboration and performance.
• I gave my one day "Process Excellence Energiser" training in Nairobi to the Medair South Sudan support office and to the Somalia office there. When I met the Somalia deputy country director six months later and asked him about the impact of the training, he said it had changed the culture. He cited the following

example: every time we think about how to do a new task or create a new process, we always ask, "How can we do this right the first time to avoid rework and delays?"

• In this "Make It Better" summary slide, a colleague used formulas in Excel to automatically copy information from one form (a stock request) onto another form (a waybill). This eliminated the need to do this manually and an opportunity to make a mistake.

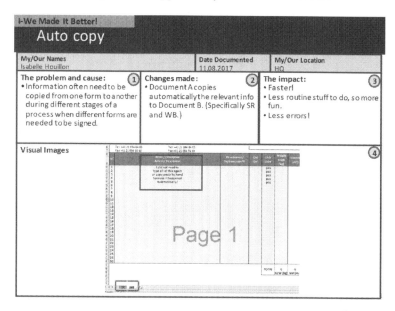

• In this "Make it Better" improvement, a colleague requested our mobile phone company (Salt) to combine invoices by department. This reduced the number of monthly invoices we receive and process from 40 to 10. And it increased the timeliness of our payments!

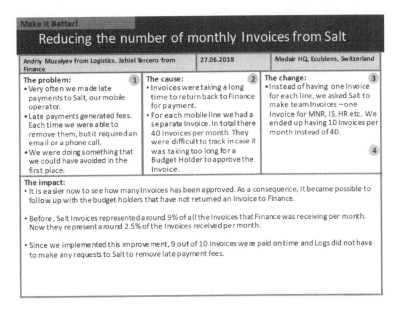

Make it Better!

Reducing the number of monthly Invoices from Salt

Andriy Muzalyev from Logistics, Jehiel Tercero from Finance	27.06.2018	Medair HQ, Ecublens, Switzerland

The problem: ①	The cause: ②	The change: ③
• Very often we made late payments to Salt, our mobile operator. • Late payments generated fees. Each time we were able to remove them, but it required an email or a phone call. • We were doing something that we could have avoided in the first place.	• Invoices were taking a long time to return back to Finance for payment. • For each mobile line we had a separate Invoice. In total there 40 Invoices per month. They were difficult to track in case it was taking too long for a Budget Holder to approve the Invoice.	• Instead of having one Invoice for each line, we asked Salt to make team Invoices – one Invoice for MNR, IS, HR etc. We ended up having 10 Invoices per month instead of 40. ④

The impact:
• It is easier now to see how many Invoices has been approved. As a consequence, it became possible to follow up with the budget holders that have not returned an Invoice to Finance.

• Before, Salt Invoices represented around 9% of all the Invoices that Finance was receiving per month. Now they represent around 2.5% of the Invoices received per month.

• Since we implemented this improvement, 9 out of 10 Invoices were paid on time and Logs did not have to make any requests to Salt to remove late payment fees.

• In this "Make it Better" improvement, another colleague added a checklist to a folder into which others were supposed to upload documents. Placing the guidance on how to upload a file right where the file is uploaded made it easier and more likely for people to read and follow it.

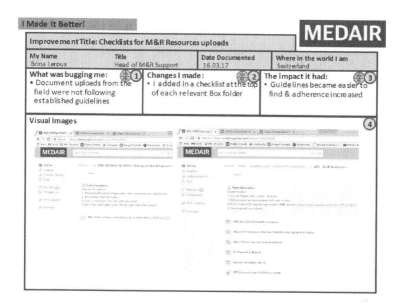

I Made It Better!

Improvement Title: Checklists for M&R Resources uploads

MEDAIR

My Name	Title	Date Documented	Where in the world I am
Brina Leroux	Head of M&R Support	16.03.17	Switzerland

What was bugging me: ①
- Document uploads from the field were not following established guidelines

Changes I made: ②
- I added in a checklist at the top of each relevant Box folder

The impact it had: ③
- Guidelines became easier to find & adherence increased

Visual Images ④

• As part of the Lean Green Belt training I conducted in Medair in Switzerland in 2018, we did some 3S/visual management in the office supplies and kitchen areas. In these before and after photos, one can see there is still room for improvement, but things are better.

*Under the sink **before***

*Under the sink **after***

*Shabby paper text labels **before***   *Heavy duty picture plus text labels **after***

*Cluttered and poorly labeled office supplies **before***   *Fewer and better labeled office supplies **after***

Medair's new CEO, David Verboom, has initiated many new changes, and he places great emphasis on simplifying work. Challenging financial realities also mean that we need to function with fewer people. I believe that the cultural changes brought about by Lean Six Sigma, and the improvements enabled by applying LSS thinking and tools, have helped provide a strong foundation for the changes that the organization is now going through.

What I benefited from the experience

Working for World Vision and Medair is rewarding to me because I am personally committed both to helping people in need and to how these two NGOs help people. By being part of an NGO, I am able to do more than send a check to an organization. I can help them 'do good better' by sharing with them my personal passion for improvement and my professional skills in Lean and Six Sigma. While I am fortunate to be able to do this as my full-time work, the volunteers who have helped us have also considered their work with us a personal highlight for themselves.

My work is not only about helping an NGO reach more people. It's also about touching the lives of my colleagues and enabling them to work more effectively and efficiently. It's about instilling in them a vision for a better way of working together (of Process Excellence) and empowering them to pursue that vision (to improve their processes) by applying the principles and practices of Lean and Six Sigma. I am always pleased to hear when improvements make their workday easier and allow them to be more productive. This has the double benefit of relieving stress on my colleagues and helping my organization to provide aid to more people suffering from crisis or conflict.

I also really enjoy when I hear stories that my colleagues tell me of how they have applied LSS outside of work. One colleague in Kenya, who is also a mother, developed a schedule of chores and meals for the family's house helper. This standard work saved time for the house helper and improved everyone's satisfaction with the meals.

Truly, Lean Six Sigma thinking and tools apply in many areas of life. Helping others to catch this vision and then helping them make improvements is exciting, especially because I help people who help make life better for others. I am honored to work as a LSS professional – among experts who have both the desire and ability to help make the world a better place, and who volunteer to help others do this with greater effectiveness, efficiency and impact.

Links to books, organizations, and my contact info for people to connect with me

- Walking with the Poor: https://amzn.to/2igBb1s

- World Vision International: https://www.wvi.org/
- My article "Improving Processes for Good in East Africa" in The TQM Journal, Volume 25, Issue 5: https://www.wvi.org/africa/publication/improving-processes-good-east-africa
- Medair: https://www.medair.org/
- Toyota's "Meals per Hour" video of how they helped a New York soup kitchen; here they also present stories of how they have helped other nonprofits: http://www.tssc.com/nfp-mph-vid.asp
- I recommend listening to this inspiring book "2 Second Lean" by Lean fanatic Paul Akers: https://paulakers.net/books/2-second-lean
- My LinkedIn profile: https://www.linkedin.com/in/andrew-parris-0b4ab28/

The nonprofit to which I will donate the book proceeds and where can others learn more about it

I will donate the book proceeds to Medair, which can be found online at https://www.medair.org/

Mark Novak: Leaning Out Disaster Relief

Lessons from Mississippi

I was approached by my daughters' Youth Pastor in 2005, who was planning a disaster relief trip to Gulfport, Mississippi to help with disaster relief after Hurricane Katrina. Feeling called to do something, and with years of do-it-yourself handyman experience, I agreed to the nine day trip without hesitation. Since it was my first service trip, I felt obliged to follow the leads of the rest of the 80-person team, taking direction from, and joining in on numerous conversations with the church's other adult leaders. It was to be an eye-opening experience.

Roughly 80 willing missioners, most of us from St Paul's United Methodist Church in Cedar Rapids, Iowa, piled into two motor coach buses and a few personal vehicles for the two-day drive. About half were under 18 - many on their first service trip - and the rest at various ages and life stages up to 84 years young. Construction skills were among the highest in need at our destination, yet those skill levels varied widely across our group. Also needed were project management skills, small group leadership talents, teaching ability and truckloads of patience.

After arriving at our Mississippi host church, the Youth Pastor and a half-dozen adult team leaders (referred to as the "skilled team") piled into a couple of cars and navigated to multiple addresses provided to us by the local relief management agency. The teams were made up of the Pastor and those most experienced at multiple types of do-it-yourself projects. In the waning light, the group assessed the storm damages, made rough estimates of material needs, and began to formulate a plan of attack to address the needs of the stricken.

9/13/2005 photo of Biloxi, Mississippi. Source: NOAA's National Weather Service

We planned to pick up materials at the local home center the next morning. The skilled team returned to camp to evaluate the availability of expertise in the larger group, and assigned missioners and leaders in groups of six to ten people to the work teams. They would go forth in the morning to the work locations to do great things with positive intent.

The work assignments came from the Federal Emergency Management Agency (FEMA), the United Methodist Council on Relief (UMCOR) and local agencies. They were all trying to coordinate a myriad of volunteer teams from all over the country, each with their own abilities and limitations. About half of the work assignments that the pastor had received a week in advance were no longer valid. Other teams had either already completed the work we were assigned, or there was incomplete work that prevented us from getting started on our specific tasks.

Day One

After getting our assignments, our work teams loaded up dozens of totes of tools onto the buses the next morning, ready to do the expected work of the day. The buses dropped groups off at our assigned work sites with tools, coolers of sack lunches, and high spirits, ready to serve the battered community. We were surprised to find out that the work needed wasn't quite what was described in the work orders, and that the tools on hand in those totes didn't seem to match the job, and that the building materials needed were slow to arrive. The one or two skilled leaders assigned to the team would then circle the property (re-assessing in daylight what was dimly seen in a few dusky minutes the night before), then organized their team members and got the work started. The work typically consisted of shingle removal and replacement, drywall installation, painting, and debris removal. By 10:00 a.m., the energetic teams had done everything they could without the needed materials. They found "busy work" to occupy themselves until their materials were delivered to the site by the supply team. The supply team had planned to pick up supplies each morning and deliver them to the work teams scattered across town. That team consisted of members of our group who had driven their own pickup trucks, along with the pastor (who had the only Church credit card).

In Biloxi, Miss., a view of the rubble in the wake of Hurricane Katrina, Aug. 30, 2005. Photo by Barry Williams/Getty Images

In the aftermath of Katrina, the local Home Depot had been demolished, but they had set up circus-sized tents as temporary stores to meet the immediate needs of the community. Other supplies were also available at the UMCOR supply depot outside of town, although the inventories were limited in quantity, selection and availability. The stores were crowded, lines were long, and supplies were short, which delayed material deliveries well past the planned time of arrival at the work sites. Incoming calls from the site leaders altered the materials orders considerably. The two or three supply team shoppers would re-circle the store to locate needed materials, missing tools and other supplies. They would then wait in long lines with contractors, other missioners and local homeowners to pay for their goods. After loading up and delivering the materials to the sites, they found the teams idle, lacking what they needed to get the job done, and somewhat frustrated at not being able to get started. Some had eaten lunch and were napping in any shade they could find. With materials finally on site, the team re-organized and put in a few hours of productive work before the bus arrived to return them to camp for showers and supper.

At the daily leader meeting back at camp, each leader reported on their progress, their team, and the issues faced during the day. Some leaders reported lacking needed skills on their teams, even having to teach volunteers how to hold and swing a hammer, use a tape measure, or mark a piece of drywall for cutting. All voiced frustration that they could have done more had they had all they needed to get started. Vowing to "do better tomorrow," we adjourned for the night.

Day Two

Day two started better for most work teams, having received at least some of the needed materials from the supply team the afternoon before. The expected duration of most of our work assignments ranged from a few hours to a few days. Planning for the next job began at the nightly leader meeting once a team leader indicated their team had already finished or would finish work at their jobsite the next day. The day went comparatively smoothly until the materials begin to run short, or when small jobs were completed (leaving a team idle until a bus arrived), or when there was an apparent mismatch in skills-to-tasks.

At the progress report that evening, leaders discussed and evaluated materials, tools and skills, and new lists were made of who needs what, where, and when. The challenge was trying to deal with changing orders from local relief authorities, teams completing small jobs and team reassignments, material replenishment needs for the bigger jobs, a shuffling of people to match skills to jobs, and many return trips to Lowe's or Home Depot to resupply the teams' needs. In the busyness, the waste is forgotten and the satisfaction of completing a few jobs is celebrated.

John Sanders of Biloxi spends a quiet moment on the once quiet, pristine stretch of Biloxi beach on September 2, 2005. Photo by Marianne Todd/Getty Images

By now, it was obvious that the work was planned poorly and organized loosely. Supplies were scare or late to arrive, and communication of problems was accomplished too late in the day. As frustrating as the "Mississippi 1" trip was, the mantra among the group had been "stay flexible and you won't get bent out of shape."

Once materials started to catch up with demand, the workflow became steadier, and the ensuing accomplishments made all of us feel that we had delivered some degree of value to the stricken communities. The work we had completed was a small drop in what we had seen to be a very large bucket of need. We observed the destruction firsthand through bus windows while traveling between camp and worksites, and in the neighborhoods surrounding our work sites.

When the decision came from church leaders the following year to return to the hurricane zone, we understood the need was still great, and we were again willing to use our gifts to provide whatever relief we could to the victims.

Mississippi 2

The next mission trip the following year (dubbed "Mississippi 2") went much the same way. During that return trip, I decided to use some of the 20-hour drive time on the bus to have one-on-one After Action Reviews (AAR) with each team leader and the Pastor. We were unanimously still frustrated, as all of us believed we could have done more good with the limited time we had in the disaster zone. Knowing these trips would be an annual pilgrimage from our church to parts of the central U.S. most in need each July, we agreed to meet in March of the following year to plan the next July trip in advance.

Working on improvements

The following spring, I shared my notes from the individual conversations with the various team members and team leaders, and we constructed a fishbone diagram to organize our thoughts around what was - and what was not - going well.

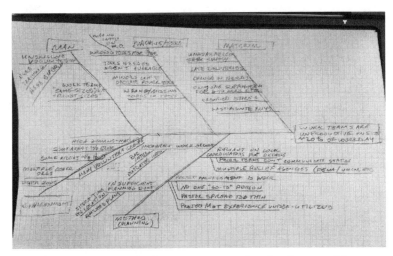

Fishbone Diagram created to brainstorm causes for why the teams felt unproductive over 20% of the day

Mission Trips: Productivity Improvement	

Problem statement:
Mission work teams are idled when on site by lack of supplies, tools and training for the work assigned.
	Countermeasures:
	1. **Experienced Project Manager is assigned**
	2. **"Advance Team" is planned to arrive on location 2-3 days ahead of main group:**
	   a. Collaborates with authorities on assignments that match team abilities
	   b. Goes to sites to assess assignments, and completes statement of work for each
	   c. Purchases or orders materials locally, and makes final tooling and equipment plans w/mission leaders prior to main group's departure

Metrics: Downtime % (estimated): Mississippi Trip #1: 20% Mississippi Trip #2: 20%	
Root Cause Analysis (from fishbone exercise): 1. Project management practices aren't used 2. Information needed is late or inaccurate 3. Supplies needed are late or unavailable 4. Tools and equipment needed are late or unavailable 5. Work teams are untrained in the work they are assigned	3. "Supply Team" has own credit cards, multiple vehicles, and is in contact with team leaders throughout the workday a. Project Manager is on this team, and visits sites repeatedly throughout the day 4. Work teams load tool totes with tools and supplies for the next day the night before 5. Missioners receive hands-on training before departure from home, or the evening prior to going on-site

A3 summary report describing the high level productivity improvements during 3rd mission trip

Key actions:

1. An experienced Project Manager was assigned, responsible for disaster relief planning, leaving the Pastor free to plan the social and spiritual aspects of the mission experience.

2. Advance team arrived two days prior to main body of missioners to meet with local authorities, scout sites to verify work progress and local conditions, and prepare initial materials and equipment lists. The team also placed orders for Day 1 materials in advance, and notified larger team of additional equipment or tools needed prior to departure from home.

3. Supply team issued multiple credit cards, used multiple vehicles (and the cargo bays of the buses) to deliver material to work sites.

4. Project bins were created with standardized tools and supplies (see Appendix) for specific tasks. Bins were verified complete on the evening before they are needed, and issued to site team leaders.

5. Basic skills training was completed one to two weeks prior to departure. On-the-job training only needed to refresh the basic training when on site.

Success!

Value was loosely defined as "making each home more habitable" with the skills we had. The changes in how we managed the volunteer disaster relief effort nearly doubled the value-added proposition of our team. We took subsequent trips to Joplin, Missouri and Moore, Oklahoma after those communities were devastated by EF4 and 5 tornadoes. The changes we adopted with the new processes enabled our teams to serve twice as many homeowners. Additional benefits included less stress on the Pastors, happier mission-goers who felt like they were able to contribute more than before, and better relationships between the church and the disaster management agencies we coordinated with.

BEFORE   AFTER

Before and after photos of Joplin, Missouri. Briarwood Elementary School is
shown in the bottom center of each photo

On a personal note, as a problem solver and "lean guy," my own
level of satisfaction skyrocketed. I was able to spend more time with
the people affected by each disaster, and happier, more productive
teams were gratifying to see as we continued to travel to where the
need was greatest in the years that followed. Each of us shared our
skills, energies and faith without the disappointing waste evident
in the earlier trips. As the "experienced project manager" assigned
after the Mississippi trips, I also remembered to teach the next
person. Knowledge isn't power unless it's also shared. The disaster
relief teams of the future can learn a lot from those who have
already been in the "eye of the storm."

Appendix - Standardized Tools and Materials List

DRYWALL INSTALLATION – STANDARD MATERIALS & TOOLS

Materials needed for drywall installation

- Drywall panels
- Drywall compound (Mud)
- Paper or fiberglass drywall joint tape
- Drywall shims
- Metal or paper-faced corner bead

- Drywall screws- 1 1/4"
- Drywall sanding screen (open grit sandpaper)
- Corner bead
- Drywall nails - 1 1/4" or 1 3/8"

Tools needed for drywall installation

- First Aid kit
- Utility knife
- Drywall saw
- Tin snips
- 6"/5" and 10" joint finishing knives
- Corner trowels – inside & outside
- Bread pan for compound
- Drywall lift or T-jack (for ceilings)
- 4' Drywall T-square
- Electric screw guns/Drills
- Screwdriver
- Phillips bits
- Dumpster/solid waste receptacle
- Nail aprons

- Drywall screw "dimpler" attachment
- Measuring tape
- Rasp
- Sandpaper
- Utility wet/dry vacuum cleaner
- Pole Sander
- Safety glasses
- Hammers
- Marking pencils
- Dust masks
- Ladders
- Scaffolding if > 8' high walls)
- Chalk lines

If there is no electricity on site, add:

- Generator and gas can
- Fire extinguisher

- Lighting
- Power Strips/extension cords

How to Calculate Materials needed:

You can determine how much material you'll need by figuring out the square footage of your room (Length times width) plus 10% (15% if you have inexperienced installers). So if you have 350 square foot room add 35 feet to account for waste. Divide this total by 32 to use 4' x 8' pieces of drywall and round up to determine the number of sheets you will need. To calculate how many supplies you'll need purchase for every 1,000 square feet of coverage, you will need: 370 feet of joint tape, 140 pounds of compound, 700 screws (or nails). (Source: http://www.doityourself.com/stry/drywall-supplies-needed-from-start-to-finish#b#ixzz37el6kMYW)

RE-SHINGLING ROOFS– STANDARD MATERIALS & TOOLS

Materials needed for roofing installation:
- Coil/Strip nails to fit types of nail guns used, nail length to meet local code
- Utility knife blades
- Roofing staples
- Roofing felt
- Roofing compound ("blackjack" in caulk gun tubes is easiest)

- Shingles
- Drip edge
- Flashing
- Roofing nails (bulk
- Vent pipe boots

If damaged wood will be replaced:
- Roof sheeting to match thickness of existing roofing material (to code)
- Construction adhesive (in caulk gun tubes)(if needed to meet code)

- 8d and 10d nails (or to local code)
- Roofing clips at sheeting thickness
- "Hurricane clips" (if needed to code)

Tools needed for roofing removal & installation:
- First Aid kit
- Roofing spades (to remove shingles)
- Push brooms
- Large tarps
- Hammers
- Utility knives w/blades
- Tape measures
- Manual or power staplers
- Chalk line
- Air compressor(s)
- Compressed air nail guns & Hoses

- Dumpster/solid waste receptacles
- Pencils/markers
- Tin Snips
- Ladders
- Safety glasses
- Safety steps (rooftop toe holds)
- Nail aprons
- Work gloves
- Knee pads
- Caulk gun

If damaged wood will be replaced:
- Circular saws w/blades
- Extension cords

- Square/roofing square

IF NO ELECTRICITY ON SITE, ADD:
- Generator and gas can

- Fire extinguisher

PAINTING – STANDARD MATERIALS & TOOLS

Materials needed for painting:
- Paint
- Roller covers
- Painter's tape
- Spackling compound

Tools needed for painting:
- First Aid kit
- Safety glasses
- Rollers
- Brushes – 2", 4" flat & 2" angled
- Hammers
- Sandpaper
- Screwdrivers – flat and Phillips
- Paint scrapers
- Clean water source
- Paint can opener
- Paint can pour spouts
- Ladders & step stools
- Paint trays
- Rags
- Putty knives
- Drop cloths (cloth or resin paper, not plastic, which slips)

You can download a PDF of these standard material lists at https://bit.ly/2zkB2DW

Author Bio and Contact Information

Mark Novak is a veteran of multiple disaster relief efforts after hurricanes, tornadoes and floods in many locations. He has been deeply engaged with lean and six sigma at Rockwell Collins for the past 15 years, where he is currently the Continuous Improvement and Next Generation Teaming Manager for the company's location in Melbourne, Florida. He continues to apply project management, lean six sigma and handyman skills in service to the Melbourne area by volunteering at the Brevard Rescue Mission (BRM)[19].

The BRM works to permanently break the cycle of homelessness in families by providing homeless women with children housing, access to health care, transportation, education, nutrition, job training and life skills in a safe, Christ-centered residential setting. The 12-24 month program is designed to lovingly transform families from dependency to self-sufficiency through daily accountability, personal responsibility and goal advancement.

---

[19]https://brevardrescuemission.org/

Proceeds from this book will be donated to this organization to help further their mission.

Mark Novak

- Email: leansixsigmaguy@gmail.com
- LinkedIn: https://www.linkedin.com/in/leansixsigmaguy/
- Twitter: @mcnovak1958[20]
- Instagram: @mark.novak.1958[21]

---

[20]https://twitter.com/mcnovak1958
[21]https://twitter.com/mcnovak1958

Brion Hurley: Applying Lean Six Sigma to a Nonprofit Fundraiser Conference

Running a small nonprofit

My entire work career has revolved around process improvement. I studied statistics and quality management in college, then worked for 18 years at Rockwell Collins as a Lean Six Sigma Black Belt. About 10 years ago, I started to transition to sustainability work, applying improvement techniques to social and environmental problems.

In 2015, I got involved in a nonprofit organization called Recycling Advocates[22] in Portland, Oregon. After a year, I was asked to take over as President of the 30-year-old organization (founded in 1987). I was new to the nonprofit board member role, so I was nervous about becoming the President. However, I figured my passion for the environment, along with the support and mentoring from other board members would help me figure out what to do.

We are a small nonprofit, so we didn't have many products or services that we offered other than education to our members. In the past, we have supported campaigns to improve recycling and other environmental causes (such as plastic bags ban, reusable beer bottles, bottle deposit bill, and e-waste regulations). Since I came on board, we have spent most of our time working on the problem of disposable and non-recyclable coffee cups.

---

[22]Recycling Advocates, http://www.recyclingadvocates.org/

However, that was also one of the challenges I had to deal with first, to make the organization more financially viable. We would ask for donations to support our causes, but it wasn't working very well. We were not bringing in enough money to cover our minimal expenses (overhead costs plus a part-time Resource Director).

One of the ideas that our board members came up with was to setup a conference and charge money for tickets.

I agreed that it would be easier to provide our members with some value for their money, instead of just asking for a donation. I was noticing that there was a lot of discussion in Portland around the topic of a "zero waste lifestyle," focusing on minimizing purchases and reducing the amount of trash being generated at home. Some people have even reduced their trash down to one bag or container per year!

In the business world, there was also a growing interest in companies becoming "zero waste" to support their sustainability programs. I recently achieved a certification as a TRUE Zero Waste Business Advisor[23]. I felt that hosting a conference to bring people together to educate them about how they can apply zero waste principles to their life would be a great idea, both for our organization and for our supporters.

But I hadn't ever setup or run a conference before, especially an event with more than 20 people with a focus on raising money for a nonprofit organization.

Since my background was in Lean and Six Sigma, I felt confident that I could use these tools and techniques to help me figure it out. I've also attended a lot of Lean Six Sigma conferences over the years, so I felt like I was experienced as a conference attendee. I have often thought about ways to improve the conference experience.

---

[23]TRUE Zero Waste Advisor, https://true.gbci.org/true-advisor

Will anyone attend?

The first thing I did was partner with someone who knew the potential audience better than I. I connected with a friend of mine to help me out, Chloe Lepeltier. She ran a Facebook group called "Zero Waste PDX"[24] and it was gaining in popularity. I pitched the idea to her, and she liked it and was interested in helping me set it up.

The next thing we did was to figure out if there was actual interest in having a conference. If there was interest, what would people want to learn?

We didn't want to waste too much effort putting on a conference that nobody wanted to attend. As with any effort, we need to know if we are offering value to our customers.

A few years ago, I read a popular book called "The Lean Startup"[25] by Eric Ries. He talks about ways you can test out your ideas first, before you design and develop a new product or service. These concepts were developed based on the principles of the Toyota Production System (which is the foundation of Lean methodology). There was another book published shortly after, explaining how these Lean Startup concepts could be applied to nonprofits in the book "Lean Startups for Social Change"[26] by Michel Gelobter. I was excited to test out these startup concepts on this conference.

We first setup an online survey, to see what kind of response we would get for our conference idea. I was confident there would be interest, but I didn't know how much interest there would be. That is the whole point of the Lean Startup approach, to get actual data on uncertain ideas from the customers and stakeholders. It's also a core principle in Six Sigma (gathering and analyzing data), so I really liked this approach.

---

[24]Zero Waste PDX Facebook Group, https://www.facebook.com/zerowastepdx
[25]The Lean Startup, https://amzn.to/2QkRgXn
[26]Lean Startups for Social Change, https://amzn.to/2PV4c6Z

After a couple weeks, we reviewed the feedback from the survey. We had about 115 people fill out the survey, which I thought was a positive response. That gave us confidence that we could get at least half of those people to attend an event.

Next, we went through the different topic ideas and comments, and tried to categorize those results into a Pareto Chart (like we often do when attempting to reduce defects in a process or prioritize our improvement work). See Figure 1 below.

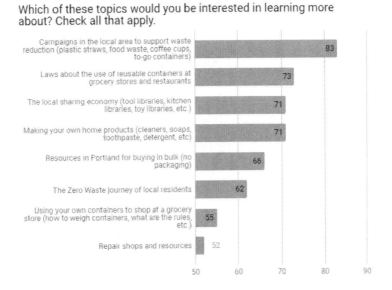

Which of these topics would you be interested in learning more about? Check all that apply.

Figure 2: Survey Responses about Potential Conference Topics

We took the top ranked categories and tried to determine who we should invite to be a potential speaker on each topic.

As we went through each category, we had a few names of people we could invite, which gave us more confidence that we could provide good value to the attendees.

We also had to figure out how long the event should be, which day of the week it should be, which month of the year it should be, and how much to charge people to attend. These questions were included in the survey.

Based on the results, we decided to charge $25 per person for a 4-hour event, to be held in the fall on a weekend during the day.

Some of these results surprised me. I was originally planning to do a full day event during the week, or in the evening during the week. However, that was not the most popular choice. That really helped guide our planning, and I think it was one of the keys to the event success.

Mitigating the risk of problems

Another powerful tool of Six Sigma is called the Failure Modes and Effects Analysis (FMEA). It is used to identify the risk of something going wrong, and mitigate the risk to reduce the chance of it actually happening. It is often used to prevent new product designs from running into problems during the manufacturing process, or when the product is being used by the end customer. However, this was a perfect tool to use in this situation, especially since it was our first time planning an event. I was really nervous that I was overlooking something that would become an issue during the event. I really wanted this event to be a great success. However, I did not want to perform a full FMEA, where you go through every single step and prioritize each risk based on severity, occurrence and detection.

Over the years of teaching, facilitating and promoting the use of FMEA's, I have found that many people like the idea of the tool, but are scared off about the time commitment required. I completely understand, as I didn't have a lot of time either, since this is all being done on volunteer time.

I've developed an approach to ease into FMEA's[27]. The idea is that you start simple by just having a discussion with others

---

[27]Tips and tricks for more efficient and effective PFMEAs, https://bit.ly/2BBAZFz

in your team, and simply ask "what are some of the risks?" As you brainstorm the risks, you discuss how well prepared you are for these risks. This exercise will help you determine if you feel comfortable with the potential risks or not, and decide if you should go deeper into your risk assessment.

If you realize that there are more risks than you thought, then the next step I recommend is to walk through the full process all the way as the customer (conference attendee), to see what their experience might be as currently setup.

First, they're going to sign up on the website, then decide how to pay, receive an electronic ticket as confirmation, travel to the event location on event day (using different transportation methods), walk to the event entrance, look for signage on where to go, check-in, and find a place to sit.

As we talked through these steps, many questions came up.

Do we have directions to the event? Do they know where to park? Do they need to bring their ticket? Was the event entrance easy to find? Do they need a name tag? Do they want something to eat or drink? Are they going to want to take notes during the event? How do they find and get into their seats? Will the aisles be spaced in a way to make it easy to get into their seats?

Finally, we tried answering these questions, and discussed ways we could mitigate the potential problem.

As an example, for the seating problem, I anticipated that people would come in later, and this would make it easier for them to quietly sit at the edges of the rows. What normally happens is that the open seats are often in the middle of a row, and people are climbing over each other and creating a distraction.

To mitigate the seating problem that I've experienced at other conferences, I created a PowerPoint slide that was rotating at the beginning that would remind people to move to the center of the seating. I also encouraged people to introduce themselves to their neighbors, so they would be more comfortable sitting next to each other.

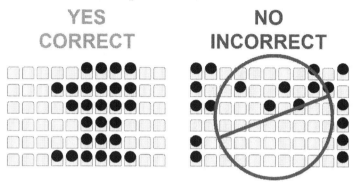

Figure 2: Slide presented to attendees to encourage better seating arrangements

We didn't have as many people show up as we were planning for, so it didn't end up being as big of a problem as I expected. A quick glance at the seating arrangement showed mixed results with the sign, so a future improvement would be to remind people during the event to move to the center.

We also thought about the speaker experience, not just the conference attendee. Where will they be standing? What digital format will they use for their presentations? Are they going to engage the audience?

After we brainstormed the questions for our risk discussion, the next decision was whether the questions and answers we came up with made us feel comfortable with the event planning so far, or raised a lot of "red flags" and concerns.

If it raised some serious questions and concerns, then it might justify performing a full FMEA. A full FMEA would require us to go step-by-step through the process, and brainstorm every potential failure we could think of, and score the risks from highest to lowest in order to prioritize what to work on. This takes a while to complete, but for large and important events, it might be worth the effort.

For our event, we felt good about the answers we had, so we didn't feel that a full FMEA was necessary. We simply listed out the questions, and the mitigation we were going to take for each risk. Here are a couple examples...

- Projector doesn't work or dies during event

** Bring 2nd projector as backup

- Credit card payment device doesn't work due to poor internet connection

** Bring 3 devices and phones as backup

- Presentation is hard to see on white screen (contrast/lighting)

** Arrive early to test and adjust lighting in room

- Room gets too hot due to number of people

** Setup fans near exits if weather looks to be warm and we have full attendance

- Attendees only have cash and want change

** Withdraw $50 in one dollar bills and bring to event

Skipping ahead, I felt like we did a great job overall with the event. There weren't any major hiccups, so I feel like we addressed or avoided many of the risks we identified, or some of them never came to fruition. The only thing we didn't consider as a failure was not having the speaker show up. We had no mitigation plan for that. Luckily, everybody showed up as expected, but that was something that we need to have a mitigation plan for next year. We also didn't have a place for the speakers to sit, which was minor, but an improvement we can make next year.

Obviously, small things came up that we didn't anticipate. But I think overall the event went pretty smoothly, so I think we did the right amount of risk assessment.

Flow of attendees at check-in

From a lean perspective, one area I was concerned about was the flow of attendees into the event space. The ideal scenario in lean is that your customer demand is consistent and steady. For this conference, that means that attendees trickle into the event in a steady flow one at a time, not all at once. Large groups can overload the process and back up the line, which makes people wait in line, and it puts stress on our volunteers.

To deal with this issue, I wanted to figure out how to help spread out the arrival times of the attendees, and keep the check-in process quick and simple.

The first thing was to avoid technology. I love technology, but I was concerned that it would slow down the check-in process, and increase the risk of something going wrong. We opted to print out 3 copies of the attendee list. We simplified the process, so all the volunteers had to do was cross off the name of the attendee, and that's it. It only took 5-10 seconds per person. It also gave us flexibility to help out if we saw the line getting longer, instead of only having one person with the list (creating an unnecessary bottleneck). We also tried to spread out the volunteers near the entrance to create more space and room. This would allow people to get around each other and go to the next check-in person who was available, and not interfere with people trying to enter the room.

I didn't actually observe anything about the sign-in process, but the feedback was good, and the volunteers said they weren't overwhelmed, so I took that as a success. One minor issue was that the name tag creation station wasn't located in the most ideal spot. Luckily, the majority of people brought their own name tags (to stay aligned with the purpose of the event), so it didn't impact the flow very much. The "bring your own name tag" program worked out really well. We minimized waste, and it ended up being a good conversation starter, especially for those who made their own fancy one, or had a unique badge from work.

Minimizing environmental impact

Here are all the things we did in our conference to reduce our impact on the environment.

- Encouraged attendees to bring their own name tag
- No printing of agendas or schedules
- Very few printed flyers for promotion, almost all was done online
- Promoted "Bring your own cup" (BYOC) and provided reusable mugs for those who forgot
- Provided reusable fabric squares made with beeswax for the snacks
- Told everyone to "Pack in, pack out" if they brought anything to the event
- Check-in with electronic tickets, not printed tickets
- Encouraged attendees to take public transportation or carpool
- Told sponsors to minimize or eliminate any handouts or freebies

Attendance Predictions

One area that was a negative was the actual attendance. We had many more sign-ups than actual attendees, and we had a waitlist, so there were people who signed up but didn't attend, and those that wanted to attend but were not able to attend. That is another problem we need to fix for our next event.

Because of my Six Sigma background, I was really interested in accurately predicting attendance numbers. Here is how we ran the event for determining capacity.

The room capacity was set at 150 people. Based on other free Lean Six Sigma workshops I've put on over the past 2 years, I had some data on attendance rate for those that register for a free event. This event is a little longer and a different topic, but it's the best data I had at the time. We also had a small sample of data from workshops where people donated money to attend, and it was 100% attendance for all 17 people.

We broke up the attendees into 5 categories, and estimated actual attendance based on sign-up numbers. Because we did not anticipate having people show up at the door who were not signed up, I added a 6th category below called "Pay at door."

Free

Free attendee signups = 20
Expected attendance based on past Lean Six Sigma workshops = 50%
Expected attendees = 10
Actual attendees = 12 (60%)

Sponsors

Sponsor allotment = 22
Expected attendance = 80% (estimate only, no data)
Expected attendees = 18
Actual attendees = 14 (64%)

Speakers

Number of speakers = 9
Expected attendance = 100% (estimate only, no data)
Expected attendees = 9
Actual attendees = 9 (100%)

Paid (donated at least $5)

Paid signups = 74
Expected attendance = 95% (based on 17/17 attendance for paid
Lean Six Sigma workshops)
Expected attendees = 70
Actual attendees = 51 (69%)

Volunteers

Number of volunteers = 14
Expected volunteers = 90% (estimate only, no data)
Expected attendees = 13
Actual attendees = 10 (71%)

Pay at door (day of event, not registered)

Number of signups = 0
Expected attendees = 0% (estimate only, no data)
Expected attendees = 0
Actual attendees = 8 (5% of room capacity)

Based on our estimated attendance, we expected 120 people, but only had 104 (including 8 people who showed up at the door), so there were far more people we should have invited from the waitlist to attend. I did want to stay under the capacity number (ideally around 140 people), but I did not want to be that far under the room capacity. In hindsight, we should have invited 30 more people off the waitlist to get us closer to 125-130 actual attendees (as 140 would have felt very crowded in that space).

That is something we will improve next time, now that we have at least one data point. As we continue to conduct these events, we can add more statistics and probability to the attendance to get even more accurate predictions.

Results

Overall, we were able to raise over 1500 dollars for Recycling Advocates. We got some of the money from sponsors, and the rest from the attendees.

That is a lot of money for our nonprofit, since we only bring in about 5000 dollars a year. It was also my first major fundraising effort since I became President 2 years ago, so this gave me a lot of confidence to put on more events in the future.

Pete Chism-Winfield presents at the Zero Waste Conference

But like everything, we could have done better. The key to establishing an improvement program within a nonprofit or for-profit business is to measure your results. Surveys are popular approaches to gather data, especially for events and conferences. We created a short survey to see how we did.

Net promoter score (NPS) is a popular way to determine if we will likely gain support and word-of-mouth recommendations for future conferences.

Although not often mentioned as a Lean or Six Sigma tool, it is a great indicator or customer metric that can drive the need for improvement.

We included one question to measure our NPS,

"On a scale of 1 to 10, how likely are you to recommend the next zero waste event to like-minded friends and family?"

Results of this question are shown in Figure 3.

On a scale of 1-10, how likely are you to recommend the next zero waste event to like-minded friends and family?

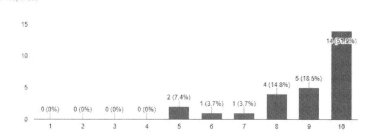

Figure 3: Results of Net Promoter Score Question

A definition of how to calculate NPS is provided by Wikipedia[28] below.

"Those who respond with a score of 9 to 10 are called Promoters, and are considered likely to exhibit value-creating behaviors, such as buying more, remaining customers for longer, and making more positive referrals to other potential customers. Those who respond with a score of 0 to 6 are labeled Detractors, and they are believed to be less likely to exhibit the value-creating behaviors. Responses of 7 and 8 are labeled Passives, and their behavior falls between Promoters and Detractors. The Net Promoter Score is calculated by subtracting the percentage of customers who are Detractors from the percentage of customers who are Promoters. For purposes of calculating a Net Promoter Score, Passives count toward the total number of respondents, thus decreasing the percentage of detractors and promoters and pushing the net score toward 0. An NPS can be as low as –100 (every respondent is a "detractor") or as high as +100 (every respondent is a "promoter"). A positive NPS (i.e., one that is higher than zero) is generally deemed good, and an NPS of +50 is generally deemed excellent."

[28]Wikipedia - Net Promoter Score (NPS), https://en.wikipedia.org/wiki/Net_Promoter

Score	Category	Count	Pct
9 or 10	Promoter	19	70.30%
7 or 8	Passives	5	18.50%
0 to 6	Detractors	3	11.10%
Total		**27**	**100%**

Figure 4: Summary results of Net Promoter Score Question

Using this definition, we calculated NPS as follows.

NPS = % Promoters - % Detractors = 70.3% - 11.1% = 59.2

Our score of 59.2 would be considered excellent. I am pretty happy with the score, but I know there is more we can do to increase the score next time.

If you are interested in watching the presentations from our event, you can check them out on the YouTube channel[29] for the event. The video recording and editing was donated by one of our sponsors (Stumptown Media Group[30]), which would have eaten into our expenses if we had to pay for it ourselves, or would not have turned out as professional as it did.

If you're involved in setting up a conference or event at work, or want to help with an event for a nonprofit organization, I hope some of the Lean and Six Sigma concepts I mentioned will be useful for you. I also hope you consider the environmental impact of your event, and consider ways to make it more "green."

If you have questions or want to attend the next Zero Waste conference, go to ZeroWasteConference.org[31], or contact me directly.

---

[29]Zero Waste Conference YouTube Channel, https://bit.ly/2Bzm26F
[30]Stumptown Media Group, https://www.stumptownmediagroup.com/
[31]http://www.ZeroWasteConference.org

Proceeds

Proceeds received from my chapter will be donated to Recycling Advocates[32], an Oregon nonprofit based in Portland that is "dedicated to creating a sustainable future through local efforts to reduce, reuse and recycle."

Contact

Brion Hurley is the owner of Business Performance Improvement (BPI)[33], a Lean Six Sigma consulting firm in Portland (Oregon) focused on sustainability. He currently teaches Six Sigma and Lean classes, facilitates lean events and kaizen workshops, performs statistical analysis, and mentors practitioners through improvement projects in manufacturing, service and office processes. He volunteers his time with local nonprofits through Lean Portland[34]. Prior to BPI, he spent 18 years at Rockwell Collins as Principal Lean Six Sigma Consultant. He is certified as a Master Black Belt and Lean Master, and has numerous sustainability certifications. He has a bachelor's degree in Statistics, a master's degree in Quality Management and Productivity, and lettered four years in football as a placekicker and punter at the University of Iowa.

Email: brion@biz-pi.com
Instagram: @brionhurley[35]
Website: http://www.brionhurley.com
LinkedIn: https://www.linkedin.com/in/brion-hurley-432192

---

[32]Recycling Advocates, http://www.recyclingadvocates.org/
[33]Business Performance Improvement (BPI), http://www.biz-pi.com
[34]Lean Portland, https://www.LeanPortland.com
[35]https://www.instagram.com/brionhurley

Kieran Mohammed: Performance Improvement journeyman; from manufacturing to government and nonprofits

Culture over tools

Peter Drucker said "culture eats strategy for breakfast."

Performance improvement requires more than just applying tools. It requires a level of mastery on how to effectively communicate with and inspire people, to create sight from insight. Performance improvement derives from innovation and innovation means value added change. To lead change effectively means teaching others how to lead as well as how to manage processes and deliver value. Leadership and culture are critical to success in performance improvement (Figure 1).

My performance improvement experience in government and non-profits relies on a focus on tools and technical approaches defined as projects. These projects are usually rendered through classroom training and activities with no tactical approaches for sustainability. The project thinking approach to attain strategic, systematic goals fails to deliver desired outcomes but seems to be the go-to model as a means to quickly fix and move on. Rarely do I see the conditioning of behaviors and habits, be it through kaizen and respect for people principles of Lean or other methods. But to understand why my experiences in government contradicts my philosophy about performance improvement required me to understand the structure, function and culture of government.

Figure 1: Performance Excellence Triad

I embrace continuous learning and consider myself a student first, practitioner second, and subject matter expert third. My performance improvement journey began as a practitioner, not in academia, and I began in manufacturing, not government or nonprofits. I was practicing performance improvement way before my Lean Six Sigma certification or the earliest of my degree ac-complishments. To speak about some of the critical to performance lessons would require that I give a bit of a historical backdrop of my journey.

From results to people focus

I worked with a factory of employees who taught me what leadership was during the grueling post 9/11 period when the World Trade Centers in New York City were struck by terrorists. In the ensuing weeks, suppliers and customers in every sector were shuttering their businesses at unprecedented rates, without warning. I was new at crisis management and as a new operations manager, things were moving too quickly for me. My job as an operations manager was quickly transforming into operations survival.

Prior to September 11th, 2001, I was a bullish, results driven, "failure is not acceptable," type leader. My staff hated me, but my bosses loved me because I made customers happy. As a traditional manager, I sought my approval from my leaders while demanding loyalty from my followers. Not to mention the halo effect that turned organizational efforts into leader recognition.

Customers wanted delivery pushed up by a week, needed an extra 500 pieces on an international shipment already prepped for the truck, I made things happen sparing no workforce emotional or physical expense. The consensus was my staff knew my bosses loved me and wouldn't dare complain. But they soon outgrew their fear. Somebody snitched.

In the aftermath investigation into my harsh treatment of staff to get productivity levels up, I complained about their lack of effort in a closed-door rebuttal meeting. I justified their outlook as jealousy because I showed up among some five, ten- and fifteen-year veterans and took the head management position away from them. I backed my philosophy and tactics of "tell sell yell" by (the few) glowing customer reviews we received. But the bosses weren't having it. They gave me a stern warning, but even I thought I was getting off easy. Then the decisive moment came when the bosses held a surprise department meeting a few hours later and all these "haters" stood there.

As I made my way to the near center of the meeting floor where my bosses stood, I gazed at some of the individuals, shaking my head. They looked down sheepishly. My boss explained the meeting was to address a "serious issue that was recently brought to their attention." He then verbally laid me out like a doormat in front of my staff, and then opened the floor up for questions and comments, and they flowed in. But what came out of their mouths was praise for my effort and desires for empathy and compassion.

I was confused but moved. I learned that day that my enemy was within. It was my perception and lack of facts that made me the toxic leader that I was. I was focused on the right goals but applying the wrong leadership. I learned that day that the meaning of these jobs to these employees was just as diverse as the staff standing in front of me. They valued their jobs differently. What mattered to one staff member was insignificant to another. In addition, what I valued as goals and desires for performance were not clear to them until they made a mistake. These leadership oversights were not apparent to me before this day and they were hurting the work climate.

People are complicated creatures and require facilitation such as personal support, trust, reassurance, value-based communication, attention, etc. They need certain things in cycles such as motivation and inspiration, downtime, recognition and challenge. To provide these things requires an understanding and application of leadership; something with which I realized I struggled.

Another debacle followed just days later when my bosses invited me back to their office for another sit down. "What'd I do now?" I asked with my back turned as I shut the door. Only to turn and realize there were eight people, all the executives, at this meeting. I thought I was going to be fired rather ceremoniously. But it was worse. I was asked to release eighty percent (80%) of my production and post production staff.

They asked me to give them a list by the morning. Eighty percent!

I had a production and post-production staff of one hundred employees. The week prior every employee got a note stating there was a zero overtime policy in place, no more paid leave for sick or vacation, and a temporary ten percent salary reduction effectively next paycheck. A few weeks earlier, the folks in accounting floated an outsourcing idea that would allow us to maintain production with 30% lesser operational cost. We had experimented with outsourcing before and I never liked the idea. As the operations manager I always argued that outsourcing created poor quality and slowed reaction to change because we were never able to effectively establish management controls from afar. Things were bad and there was no positive aspect in sight.

I was up all-night thinking about what I was going to do. After the "group meeting" (as I affectionately refer to my public lynching a few days prior), staff began sharing personal stories with me and I began to feel badly about the whole situation and was very disappointed in myself. All I could think about was that my grandparents were factory workers. What if they had a boss like me? I was torn up. I went back into the office. They asked for my list and I told them I didn't have one.

"You think this is a game?" the President asked. "Look, if you can't decide I'll let Jerry (the accounting manager) decide and his formula is cost based." The CEO responded hinting that I would be the top name on the list then. In this company at this moment, quality was measured in terms of cost reduction.

The President and CEO were a father and son duo. They spoke one after the other, single sentence at a time like a rehearsed script. I quickly explained that we can stagger the workforce. I grabbed a piece of paper off the printer and a pen. I drew a circle and said right now we have a standard workday, every person, eight hours, thirty minutes unpaid lunch and your floor ladies, the sewing room supervisors, get two fifteen-minute paid coffee breaks.

"Not anymore," Jerry replied. "We can then reduce hours by three or four every day or couple of days, but break this into two shifts?" I continued as I drew some small circles and filled in some data. "What about raw materials?" Jerry interrupted. "I'll take responsibility to reduce that by twenty percent," I said without thinking about it. "Twenty percent!" exclaimed Jerry with a grin of defiance. I was not sure if he was poking fun because he had already submitted a 30% reduction proposal, or just needling me because what came out of my mouth sounded asinine.

My bosses looked over at me with the entire executive team almost simultaneously waiting for my paper and pen drawing to follow for that one. None followed. Then the questions came.

"How Kieran? We've been running this plant for fifty years before you got here, how will you reduce the cost by twenty percent?"

Another followed by the office manager, another accountant, "Forget how, how long will that take you?" Accountants, geez.

Working with staff and suppliers to address the financial difficulties

The CEO butted in, "he hasn't thought it through but as soon as he starts working on it, he will let us know, right Kieran?" "Right," I

replied appreciating my boss's vote of confidence. "And also, Jerry
has some mock ups on the comparison for outsourcing that you
need to compare your strategy to as well," remarked the CEO. The
vote of confidence feeling disappeared as I now realized that they
were calling my bluff.

I did not know how to solve the problem, but I knew what their goal
was. Reduce cost to survive. My goals were to keep my staff, keep
the work internal where we can more effectively control quality
and cost, and keep satisfying customers. I returned to my desk
and called all the remaining suppliers and some of our local area
customers. I asked all of them for help and suggestions. Asking
for help before this moment was inconceivable by me, a sign of
weakness and incompetence. Now this request was for others not
me, this was bigger than my ego. Over the next few days, I met
with some of the vendors and customers. Most of them said they
were trying to solve the same problem. I invited a few of them to
have lunch. We got together and talked about the terror attacks
and everything else except business. We were avoiding the obvious.
Then Ira, "the thread guy" asked a question. "Kieran, what can we
do to help you?"

"You probably don't know this but we're your only supplier in the
North East now, we know we need each other to survive. Let's
figure out how to survive?"

It became apparent that no one had any real answers other than
to look at existing contracts a bit closer for opportunities to reduce
costs or improve outcomes. It was not a convincing strategy, but it
was the only option we can think of at the time for mutual benefit.

I went back to the executive team and explained that we can
restructure our contracts with key stakeholders, order in smaller
batches, but commit to the same quantities as before and eliminate 80% of inventory instead of 80% of staff. I had made initial
connections and set the stage for the strategy. The sales team and I
communicated and worked out deals with almost everyone, FedEx,

UPS, LTL couriers, corrugated box suppliers, and fabric mills in Mexico. We were even buying back unsold goods from our "mom and pop" retailers and in quick turn-around, selling them off to other bulk buyers like Ross stores and Daffy's.

For the short term, it went well. Commitments were made and the networking created sales opportunities for close out type deals that helped us improve cash flow to maintain operations and keep throughput going. Profit margins slimmed but we were operational. During the next three years we were able to continuously feed off this new organizational strategy of cost reduction and maximum throughput through a network system, while the external sales team sought new business in the Middle East and Asia.

Internally, we moved machines around, and analyzed anything that was costing money to operate. We were one of the first organizations to take advantage of the government's new "green" initiatives switching out our light bulbs for less heat producing, more energy efficient ones. We began using higher quality oil and fuels for our machinery that got us into rebate programs.

I cross-trained employees and began coaching employees on how I anticipated and caught errors in their processes. I began to train the workforce to be more committed to standards. In the beginning, new processes were difficult to maintain. For example, a simple process adjustment of using a shorter, single piece of shipping tape from a dispenser required management effort. We realized we did not need three pieces of eighteen-inch carton tape for our boxes. Our average shipping weight was five pounds and one piece of tape can secure a box with a weight of thirty pounds. The savings mounted to thousands of dollars over the course of a year for reinforced adhesive carton tape. However, as simple as it may seem, to get employees to stop at one piece of tape required more than just telling them to do so. Signs were placed at the taping stations reminding of the new process, and I eventually had the factory technician adjust the machine so that only the eighteen-inch dispenser button worked. Each time an employee would tell

me that the tape machine is broken, I knew a reminder was needed
because they were hitting buttons they were not supposed to. I kept
a mental note of the machine is broken complaints to gauge how
well the staff were adjusting. It went from about five per day to
zero in about one month. It took one month to have zero defects in
that particular process!

I focused on the power of people and success by network. Soon I had
other employees assigned to training and peer support activities. I
made sure everyone understood this was a group effort. Against
the wishes of the executives, we had to make some long-term
commitments with suppliers to make things happen in the short
term. Suppliers were willing to preserve long-term relationships for
short-term concessions at a time when no one seemed to be lasting
long term. It was based on trust but risky. However, the attitude
was that it kept them in business as well.

I realized through this experience and the customers we served,
what value creation looked like. Every time we aligned with our
customer requirements, we were able to reduce costs somewhere. It
became engrained in me because it was like discovering the cure for
deficient performance. Not performance in silos but organizational
performance. Produce what customers needed, when it was needed,
and using only what was needed.

Back then, I was passionate about results, still am today, but I see
results as something different from most others. I see results as
a process because results come from somewhere. I began to say
things like the "results process" instead of just the process, because I
wanted all the staff to understand that the results were outcomes of
the processes they performed. I have molded my leadership style to
a qualitative approach akin to a blended servant-transformational
style. Leadership and performance improvement are conjoined.
However, leadership as a process is not the same as being a leader.
This has become a focal point of mine when getting to the root
cause of many-failed performance improvement initiatives.

Many managers and leaders see results as only a lag outcome
of a process. Something that is produced, and by the standard
definition they are correct. But performance excellence requires an
understanding of the path to results in order to improve the results.
I focus on culture driven outcomes where results look more like
improvement in behavioral conditions. Setting up for the desired
outcomes is just as critical to me as the outcomes themselves.
There should be a people driven or behavioral outcome aligned
to process and product-based outcomes. In other words, develop
a culture that fosters the desired performance outcomes. Yet, too
often, strategies focus on isolated processes rather than systematic
performance. Desired results from these initiatives will be short
lived, if experienced at all. I focus on the lead factors to produce
the lag outcomes. When I see the people beginning to change how
they react to situations, I know the tangible outcome changes are
next to follow.

Involving the people who do the work is critical to success

Removing confusion with Lean and Six Sigma

I learned from my mistakes over the years, especially during my first year as a newly minted Black Belt back in 2009. I would introduce Lean and Six Sigma as a new subject alongside the problem we were trying to solve. Thereby creating two problems to solve. Alternatively, I would use the Lean Six Sigma methods on my own and then attempt to explain the findings and the process to a team unfamiliar with the method, only to feel frustrated due to lack of progress and digression. As the years went by, I focused on communicating to connect and deliver value content rather than expect the audience to adapt. It was easier for me to adapt my teaching style to the audience.

I focus on mastery of the practice and the philosophy of performance improvement and therefore spend a lot of time on application and outcomes using people focused simulations that require smaller teams and more individualized attention. I introduce tools to add clarity or move closer to a solution by studying and learning from cause and effect, correlations, 5 Why's, etc. By focusing on value creation, performance results are sustainable and systematic through continuous learning and improvement for both process customers and end users. Lean is best as a culture change (or conditioning) deployed enterprise wide through effective coaching and learning at the point of action or gemba, through work simulation and job training. The deployment must have a continuous network of leadership support extended throughout the organization.

Lean is about solving value deficiency problems using the most powerful problem-solving force on the planet, PEOPLE, not the tools. The tools enable empowerment and if they do not, they do not add value. Why? Because accountability and responsibility are easily assigned to tools when things do not go right. Part of the respect for people in Lean is accountability and responsibility established through empowerment. I've seen organizations so hamstrung by the tools that a consultant left behind that the teams just disregarded the whole initiative. They went back to their old ways of operation and deemed Lean and its toolkit a failure after investing a significant amount of money to improve their performance.

We've all heard "with great power comes great responsibility." I coach Green Belts to focus on team development in conjunction with tool deployment. I also coach new Black Belts on effective leadership or (soft Lean as I like to call it). They usually get confused because they love the toolkit (process mapping, SQDCM boards, Kaizen, PDSA, etc). I spend my time showing them how to make the team "tool masters" without giving up the responsibility and accountability of being the problem solvers.

Do I have a favorite tool? 5 Why's and H is the most useful and incredible value-creating tool in the toolbox, and it is a natural fit to effective communication, so I use that a lot working with nonprofits and government agencies.

I also stay away from a heavy focus on statistics (where possible) and use data to generate human activity, not generate human activity around data. My goal is always to help as many people (employees, business leaders and customers) experience value as they desire, not as an imposition upon them to which they force-fully have to conform. Most people do not gravitate to statistics in the environments within which I work. My constant focus is to create a work climate that nurtures learning, not fear of change and difficulty. If my team does not like statistics and it is necessary, I task myself with finding a solution. I have learned that technical training may not always be the best first step.

Improvement work in government

I struggle to communicate with leaders in government about per-formance. Not because we do not agree but because they feel pigeon holed by regulations, and external factors that help mold the internal operational culture. Eventually against better judgement, they compromise and set aside performance for action. Any performance activity is bottled into siloed projects that rarely produce any sustainable results. "As long as we're doing work, I feel like we're moving in the right direction," one leader quipped in response to a more performance driven approach to program function. They feel like they must live with the current conditions and there is no way around it. Usually they have no solid data other than some policies that show what they must conform to, and then they focus on what they cannot do. Instead of this defeatist approach to their decision-making, I resort to transitioning their thinking to what can be done and explore those options. I help them to readjust their focus to explore the available resources, time, human capital, etc. Forget the bright shiny object that is a can't have.

My role in government is an internal performance consultant. I work on projects such as liaising with external consultants or nonprofit vendors seeking to deploy improvement processes or new programs, training and coaching leaders, team development and process improvement.

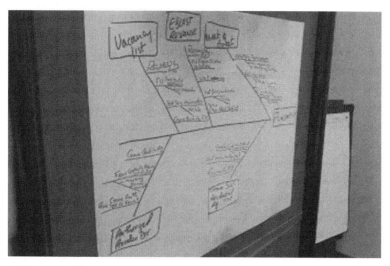

Figure 2. Fishbone Diagram used with a State agency to improve efficiency

Though I talk very little about the tools, they play a big role in team integration. While working with a team to re-engineer a complex state-run program that facilitated the housing and facilitation of disabled adults, I used the above Ishikawa diagram (Figure 2) to help a team analyze a process and eliminate a few redundant steps. We had started with a process map but the discussion got very intricate (and heated), so we created the Ishikawa, which allowed us to "punch out" the specific piece of the process that was causing some confusion and look at the minutia in isolation. A fun note was that a room full of Administrative level adults spent about five minutes repeating the word "Ishikawa" and giggling once I introduced the diagram as a "Fishbone or Ishikawa" diagram.

Figure 3. Paper House team building exercise

I serve as a State leadership team trainer on project management. The goal is to help leaders complete projects and resolve team dynamic issues more efficiently and effectively. As part of this training we do an in-classroom exercise called the paper house. The teams consist of 3 to 5 members. Each team gets a sheet of paper, which cannot be cut into multiple pieces. It must remain as a single sheet of paper. They are given a budget of $10 to purchase supplies that include: video instructions ($6), a pair of scissors ($2), adhesive tape ($2), additional paper ($1) and markers ($1). And, they have 15 minutes to complete the project which is a paper house as their final product (as shown in Figure 3).

Using an exercise like the paper house and running a decision-making simulation brings to the surface many different opinions on how to allocate resources and how to distribute responsibility. In past engagements the teams realized that with the clock ticking effective decision making about the adequate use of resources was not easy. Many teams spotlighted the current organizational culture by arguing in defiance after a failed attempt. It was interesting to see how successful teams made effective decisions that led to more efficiency and effectiveness, while the unsuccessful teams found ways to transfer the blame.

Figure 4. Nonprofit team working on Kaizen project (this was the process mapping phase)

In Figure 4, a team of nonprofit staff was engaged in a value streaming session as part of a process improvement initiative. The team needed to improve a process that used State funds to help deliver heating and air conditioning equipment to needy families. The processes were lengthy, and the program was not meeting the desired outcomes. I was asked to work with this team to help them solve these process inefficiency problems.

Figure 5. Everyone is a leader

Every member got to take the leadership role for their activities
and field questions on value creation, quality and standardization.
When there were "gaps" we "red marked the area" for review by
the entire team. As you can see in Figure 5, they had just started,
and they were "red marking" (using the pink post-its) seemingly
everything! The results returned 33 opportunities for improvement,
including reducing overall time from 45 days to 30 days, and
requiring less administrative processing of documentation due to
process redundancy.

Figure 6. Communication mapping

Figure 6 captures a communication map. I was working with a State Division on a process mapping session and something strange happened. After writing the first step "START" of the process map sitting on a table in the middle of the room, I asked," What's next?" and the room went silent. No one knew for sure how processes were initiated. The process starters were evidently not in the room.

I then went to the whiteboard and had them name all the SIPOC (Suppliers, Inputs, Process, Outputs, and Customers) entities. Once that was done, the conversation started to open up. The problem was that the individuals received directives from multiple sources. Each directive had a different process path. Each path was defined by the funding source (for which there were about twenty) and some of them overlapped, integrated or were controlled externally.

Then as the conversation evolved, we identified a more pressing problem and began a simple communication map. We were able to rank the communication and identified areas of communication inefficiency between the fiscal unit and management and the vendors and management. When we used the 5 Why's technique to explore the inefficiencies, we found that fiscal and management designed a process for the procurement unit to use that did not align with the procurement value stream or "language." The system was developed using financial codes when procurement used NAICS codes. Leaders were relatively new to the organization. However, they were delegating instructions and were never trained, nor did they inquire about processes or policies.

Summary

My journey from an operations manager in manufacturing to a performance improvement consultant and program analyst in government has provided me with a unique set of values that I apply to my performance improvement initiatives. Performance excellence, regardless of industry, should be people centered. I differentiate my approach from many Lean Six Sigma professionals by my leadership and people centered approach. I tend to stress the philosophy and the culture driven aspects of performance improvement. My early years taught me that the true emphasis for performance success relies on the development of and collaboration with people. My personal performance improvement values are based on Respect, Patience and Humility.

Proceeds

Proceeds received from my chapter will be donated to The Water Project. They are a non-profit organization with a mission of unlocking human potential by providing reliable water projects to communities in sub-Saharan Africa who suffer needlessly from a lack of access to clean water and proper sanitation. Learn more at https://thewaterproject.org/.

Contact

Kieran Mohammed served in a myriad of business sectors as a performance improvement practitioner for two decades. He holds a Doctorate in Business Administration, and Lean Six Sigma Black Belt certification. He also holds a Master of Business Administration (MBA) in Operations Management, and Accounting and Finance. He is currently the president and principal consultant at Lean Delaware, a Lean coaching and performance excellence firm. He is the author of Principles of Small Business. Kieran has served as keynote speaker on topics such as Lean thinking, Performance improvement in government, and Innovation. In 2019, he was selected to serve on the National Baldrige Board of Examiners.

Email: leandelaware@gmail.com

Brent Weichers: Training and Implementing Lean with a Blind Workforce

Background

I have been in the field of Continuous Improvement for over thirty years. I am a Lean Six Sigma Master Black Belt with a background in the automotive, aerospace, electronics and machining industries. I began my career at Toyota, and the bulk of my career was spent with Danaher, owners of Beckman Coulter, Tektronix and Fluke Instruments. I am currently the Director of Continuous Improvement at The Lighthouse for the Blind, Inc. based in Seattle, WA. They are a not-for-profit Aerospace and Military Supply manufacturing company with almost 500 employees in three manufacturing locations across the USA.

It started as a social organization called the Seattle Association of the Blind in 1914. People who were blind, along with their friends and family members, wanted to advocate to local officials regarding education, transportation, employment, and economic matters.

With the advent of World War I, many recently blinded veterans were returning home to the Pacific Northwest with virtually no opportunities for employment. A group of socially prominent women in the community helped to establish a shop in 1916, where people who were blind could make jigsaw puzzles and baskets by hand.

On April 2, 1918, The Lighthouse for the Blind, Inc. was incorporated, and began changing the lives of people who are blind, Deaf-Blind, and blind with other disabilities. In this original location, employees also manufactured brooms and sold them door to door.

The Lighthouse has been at its current location just east of downtown since 1967. With a major expansion in 1980, we have now expanded to include facilities in Spokane, Washington and Summerville, South Carolina.

Currently, Lighthouse employees manufacture aerospace parts, office products, and a myriad of other machined products for customers such as Boeing, Northrop Grumman and the Federal Government, including the US Military. We provide administrative services for customers like the U.S. Navy and manage Base Supply Center stores for several military bases. 2019 sales are expected to hit $100 Million.

The Lighthouse currently employs more than 260 individuals who are blind, DeafBlind, or blind with other disabilities. 70% of people who are legally blind are unemployed or under employed in this country.

Legoland

When I started at the Lighthouse, I soon discovered that the old ways of analysis, training and implementing Lean was not going to work here. Besides starting on the very basics with management, we had to re-invent what is normally considered a very "visual" science, and turn it into something that an employee who is blind could not only comprehend but use.

As we began getting our direct employees and management trained on Lean, the methods that most of us have used our entire careers just wasn't going to work with this population. PowerPoint slides and training manuals were the usual arsenal. This had to be translated or modified so that a blind employee could comprehend what was being taught, and participate in the process.

I have used many methods to teach the basics of batch vs flow production over the years. The Paper Airplane Folding Game, The Signature Game, and the Kanban Pizza Game. The Pizza game is a good Kanban teaching method and it is easy to transport, as it is just Post-it notes and markers. Like the other activities, it depended on eye-hand use to run the simulations, which left our blind workforce out of the exercises.

Therefore, anything that was strictly visual had to be abandoned or modified. Something I started using in the late 80's was my son's Legos (for something other than being found in the middle of the night under my bare feet). I called it The Lego Factory. During a Zombie Apocalypse, toss a few of these Legos around your doors and windows, nothing is getting past these things!

The same rules apply to the Lego Factory as the airplane folding and the signature game. You start building your lot of five, slowly reducing your lot sizes and the process accelerates. You have a lot more variation so the opportunities to improve in the training gives the trainees more to work with. The process is very tactile. Our employees can feel the different blocks and the orientation of the work in process, so they are a part of the entire learning experience. On the plus side you get to buy Legos in bulk, get a Lego VIP card. Best of all, put Legos on your expense report and drive your accountants nuts.

During the Lego Factory, I keep track of each round measuring time, cost and productivity. Getting the trainees to think about the amount of touch time and the lack of flow.

I also keep a historical record of the different teams and how they stack up because people are competitive by nature, and they usually ask how they compare.

Lean Braille Bingo

A lot of people on the shop floor have a difficult time staying focused during a training, so I introduced Lean Bingo. They pay attention and constantly ask questions trying to get me to "say the word" they need to complete their game card and get the prize, chocolate. The terms can be easily changed and used for other trainings. A random generator makes each card unique.

Since I wanted all my fellow employees to be a part of the activities I created a transferable version of the Bingo game. This Microsoft Excel version was translated to Braille by our in house team.

Once the basic concepts were taught, one of the first improvements we went after was 5S in areas that are customer critical.

LEAN INTRO B I N G O

COQ	QUALITY DEFECTS	CONTINUOUS FLOW	PARETO	HEIJUNKA
SYNERGY	OPERATOR BALANCE	ROI	STREAMLINE	ONE PIECE FLOW
CYCLE TIME	DFMEA	FREE!!!	PARADIGM	CAUSE & EFFECT
BIG PICTURE	POLICY DEPLOYMENT	MISTAKE PROOF	CELL	STANDARDIZE
RUN TIME	PUSH SYSTEM	IMPLEMENTATION	WASTE	TAKT TIME

As we know, 5S is basically the science of "what do I need and where does it go."

What I found interesting is at home, most of our blind employees were very organized by necessity. But at work, management had failed to give them the tools to be as organized at work.

Visual Workplace

The pegboard is usually a good organizing system, with the right hooks and fixtures. They are painted blue to add contrast for the employees with some sight. For most businesses it would be fine, add a little outline for the tools, and you have a working system. But for a blind employee this is nearly impossible. Are all my tools present? Are they returned to the proper location?

We have used many foam products, heavy duty closed cell foam for heavy shop tools to a light packaging foam for in-drawer layouts. This layout has the tools as they are used, from right to left in order of use. The bins hold the tooling bolts off the bench. This layout was designed with the help of a DeafBlind CNC Machine Operator.

Another product used to "set" tools in place is a material called Kaizen Foam. In this example, we have the tools set in a special foam that is layered. As the cut outs are made, you peel layers away until the depth required is reached. The Kaizen Foam comes with framing material. This is used extensively in areas that have tools of multiple depths, as the layers of foam make it easy to peel out just what is needed.

When you are required to have manuals on a shelf, one way to track if one is missing is to mark them as you can see in the photo. They are marked with a diagonal piece of tape, so when one is missing or in the wrong order, it is very obvious. We include tactile or Braille tape, so a blind employee can track books and manuals. As you can tell this is an old photo. When is the last time you saw a phone book?

In high traffic areas such as our lunchroom, we used vinyl flooring with a pattern. Our employees can find their way using a cane easily on this path. Yellow tactile guidance is used in areas that might typically be marked out in paint or floor tape, but that won't work for our employees. They have a hard time with wayfinding using only a cane and feeling for the tape.

We starting using Diamond Plate material cut to 4" widths, then painted it bright yellow. Our employees feel the bumpy plate with their canes, and for those with sight, the bright yellow is easy to follow. Double-sided tape holds it down, and it is easy to move when a change is required.

Work stations at most factories where I worked looked something like this. Lighthouse was no different. They are cheap, easy to set up, and easy to move. However, for us and for most factories, they require more time from a production lead or material handler, as there are no Kanban triggers and no 5S controls.

We started to develop our skills using Creform, a material most organizers are familiar with. We actually purchase it from several companies including NIS and Flexpipe.

A simple bench or table for a sighted employee may be fine, but it allows variation in where things are located.

With a station designed per task, our employees are more independent, as the incoming and outgoing product has specific lanes or guides. It has been ergonomically designed for the task. The parts and tools are always in the same place, as it is designed that way. Everything is fixtured, but how does a blind employee trigger a Kanban?

In this example, the bins slide down the rails towards the employee. When a bin is empty it goes down another slide towards the rear for a material handler to pick up. A sensor sees the bin and triggers a material handler to replenish it with a yellow light, and in some cases a text message.

Two bins generates a red light. The green button you see here is an andon signal.

This is a two station design, part one on the left, part two on the right.

The first employee assembles the valve, the second employee bags it with several other parts. Both have access to the andon light, and there is a slide for empty bins on each station. On the left, you see a sensor at end of slide. The empty bin is placed here, and gravity takes it to the end to trigger the sensor, and make a pick up easy for the material handler.

On the left, the finished product goes down a slide into the shipping box. The rails again are guiding the bag to the box.

In the example below, the station was designed for a DeafBlind employee. When the employee filled the bin, he bumped the lever with his foot, gravity takes the full bin to the section to be picked up. Sensors are used to notify the leads when more bins or materials are needed.

In the example below, an employee required special lighting and the use of a CCTV system. We created a light box using LED lights with a remote. We built a table around the box and installed the CCTV. Now the employee uses the CCTV to read documents and inspect product that is also backlit.

This is our home grown version of a speaking andon light. We 3D print the shell. The internal components are easily available. The front switch causes the device to vibrate three times, light the post blue, then plays a tone and speak the pre-recorded message.

The side switch is for emergencies. It lights the post red, vibrates several times and plays a European Siren. It gets your attention.

This system is inexpensive to produce, and should be used in any work area that is difficult for a production lead or supervisor to see.

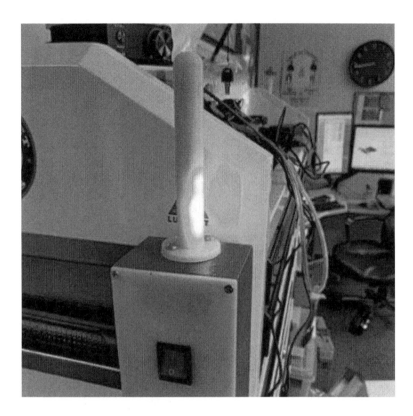

Operation MOLLE

We were making incremental improvements by training employees and getting good systems in place. But to date, we had not had a huge challenge from a customer.

MOLLE (pronounced MOLLY) is an acronym for Modular Lightweight Load-carrying Equipment. Molle uses rows of heavy-duty nylon stitched onto the vest/pack to allow for attachment of various MOLLE-compatible pouches and accessories.

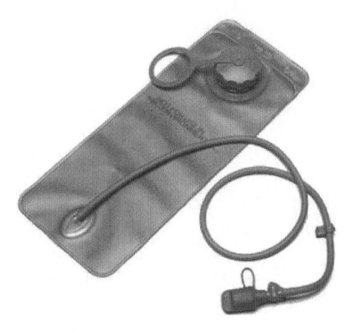

At the Lighthouse, we manufacture several versions of the Molle Bladder for the US Military. The Molle product is a very important piece of business for us. We were manufacturing 1500 units per day of this drinking bladder. We mold the plastic for the valves and caps, then purchase the bladder material, cut and RF Weld the bladder together, assemble the product, then package it in several variations. The product was easy to manage, as it was "steady eddy," always producing 1500 a day, with a takt time of 3 minutes. It was profitable. Then customers do what they always do, change the pace.

Measure	1500 Plan	2600 Plan
# of Employees	15	33
# of Blind Employees	7 of 15	14 of 32
Production per Day	1500	2600
Sq Ft	1600	1600
Cost Annualized	$662,140	$1.5 Million

When the customer requested a rather large increase in production, from 1500 a day to 2600 per day (what we call a nice problem to have), we were very excited. Then it hits the team. There was no room to add more people. If we add a second shift, we would also need room for the support staff as well. The team had little experience with Lean, but we started with the basics of flow and layout. Looking for the elusive wastes of transporation, inventory, motion, waiting, overprocessing, overproduction and defects (TIM WOOD). The old design was not able to handle the new rates. Batching was taking place using the yellow tubs (seen in the background of the picture below).

Folding tables were used temporarily, and employees were making room where they could. Up to 14 tubs were being moved around at any one time, full of products at different stages of production, but there was zero flow. All process steps were divided into "groups" or "teams." With the thought that this would be more productive, the larger the batch, the faster the flow, right? But as we started to analyze the current state, and attempt a few proposed layouts, still many of the employees were left out of the process.

We used the traditional Operator Load Chart, and we tried out different proposals, but our employees couldn't see the chart.

So again, back to the Lego store. After several layouts with the employees done in Legos, we ran a few scenarios. Like usual, we kept track of the performance in Excel, which again is not fun for a blind employee to be a part of the process. That is when Lego Excel came into play. The employees were again part of the decision to choose the layout that performed the best to takt time. With each step of the process becoming more fun and inclusive to our blind employees, the ideas started coming.

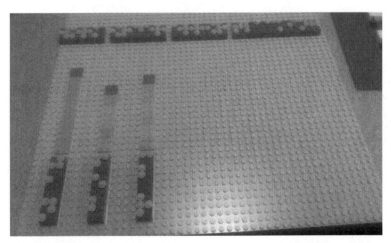

The green blocks above are Lego Braille. The Lego Braille concept was recently picked up by the State of Washington for teaching children braille letters with Legos.

We also used the Standard Worksheet, or Spaghetti Diagram as some call it. Again, when only performed on paper or computer, most of our employees didn't have a way to share input into the improvement process.

After yet another trip to the Lego store, the employees used mats and blocks to represent the pieces of equipment, benches and people in the process. Now we were all equally involved in the process of designing a new layout. To replace the tubs, we ordered a conveyor. The custom benches are shown up against the conveyor.

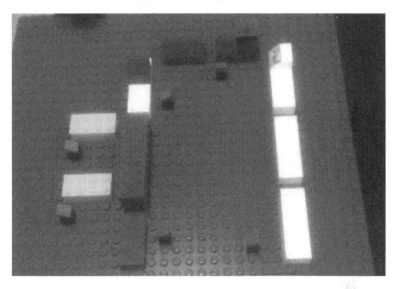

The employees take one Molle bladder, bag it, and drop it on the conveyor. It bypasses the three material handlers it used to take to move the tubs around all day. The stations in the photo can have two employees working face to face. We are using sensor technology that allows an employee to trigger a Kanban just by moving a bin. When two bins of material are present, the sensors trigger a green light, letting the lead know they are full.

When one bin is removed, a yellow light is triggered, letting the lead know a refill is needed. When both bins are removed, a red light is triggered, letting the lead know we are now in a line stop condition. There are three stations installed with two employees at each.

The sealing machine was replaced with a powered version, and the scale has been modified to speak, so the employee knows when to tape the box shut. The packaging station was a sighted job. The sealer design has a fixture with a conveyor that allows for a blind employee to seal the bag to specification. The second employee picks up the bag and adds them to the shipper.

Measure	Pre-Event	Post-Event	Gains
# of Employees	15	7	53% Reduction
# of Blind Employees	45%	100%	55%
Production per Day	1500	2600	73% Improvement
Production per Employee	100	371	271% Improvement
Sq Ft	1600	245	1355 Sq Ft
Cost Annualized	$662,140	$309,120	$353,020

Summary

What did we learn? From the improvements, we developed a formula or Standard Work that we use when coming into a a work area, which includes how and what we measure, and how we look at work stations.

We also developed the labor-reducing kanban triggers, and challenged the paradigms of what employees are capable of doing. We trained employees to understand the concepts, and tasked them with giving input on the process KPI Boards. However you decide to broadcast your results, you need to get them out there for the employees to understand how they are doing. We are always thinking of fun ways to share success by awarding teams with silly trophies or donuts when targets are met. Gemba Walks are critical to get out there on a regular basis to ask employees "what would make your job easier?" Then give them the resources they need.

Proceeds

Proceeds received from my chapter will be donated to The Lighthouse for the Blind, Inc. They empower people who are blind, DeafBlind, and blind with other disabilities by creating diverse, sustainable, and meaningful employment opportunities. Learn more at https://www.thelighthousefortheblindinc.org.

Contact

Brent Weichers has over 30 years of Toyota and Danaher experience as a Lean and Six Sigma Sensei. He is a change management expert with a keen ability to pinpoint areas for improvement, lead teams through multi-phased initiatives, and deliver measurable and sustainable results. His specialties include conducting White Belt and Green Belt training programs, leading Kaizen activities, developing and training Lean programs for all levels of an organization.

Email: BWeichers@lhblind.org

Philip Washburn: Improvement in Affordable Housing Development

A Path to Process Improvement

Some of our most life changing events happen when we least expect it. My daughters wanted to learn how to play tennis, so we signed them up for a summer camp in the evenings. There really can be no other explanation for why I would be sitting out in the hot and humid Ohio sun on a summer evening. But I took it as a chance to catch up on some reading while I waited for the class to be over.

This particular day, I was reading a book about Action Learning Teams. Throughout my career, both in the for-profit sector as a restaurant general manager, and predominantly in the non-profit sector, I have been a natural problem solver, change agent, and improvement guy. Without much formal training, I would read a lot and learn by doing. I had recently transitioned to a new role as Program Director for Habitat for Humanity-MidOhio, one of the more than 1200 local Habitat for Humanity affiliates in the US.

I realized very quickly in this new role that we had a lot of needed improvements to make us more sustainable. Our organization has multiple departments that work on various aspects of our programs, so my job was to get them to function well together. Given how different each department tended to view our work, this was an uphill battle. As I sat there reading about Action Learning, another dad approached. We started talking about the book, our kids, and business. The kind of conversation many of us have while waiting around for a class to be done. We discussed some of the problems I was thinking about, and the overall challenges of improving processes. He then, as almost an afterthought, mentioned that I should look into Lean Six Sigma, a group of process improvement tools he uses regularly in his role in Research and Development (R&D) at a large manufacturer in the area.

A few days later, I finally did a search and started to learn about Lean Six Sigma. As if a fog was finally lifted, I couldn't believe what I was reading. Each tool I read seemed like it had such potential to help us as an organization. I began to look at how to best learn about these tools, and found out about Black Belt certification. Unfortunately, the price points I was seeing were beyond my personal budget, and would have been a huge challenge to work into our non-profit operating budget.

But after a little bit of searching, I found out one of the premier online training and certification organizations for Lean Six Sigma, responsible for training Black Belts and Master Black Belts from many Fortune 100 companies, was right in our backyard. I reach out to Moresteam, and thanks to a generous scholarship, I was enrolled in their Lean Six Sigma Blended Black Belt program.

First Steps

My first steps in using the Lean Six Sigma principles to improve our processes was through improving our Home Repair program application process. Habitat for Humanity is well known for building affordable new homes around the world, something we have done very well for over 40 years. But after the housing crisis, there quickly became a realization that just building more new homes wasn't sufficient to stem the tide of people falling into substandard housing.

Many low income or fixed income homeowners lost their homes during the housing crisis, not because they were foreclosed on, but rather they were not able to affordably maintain their homes in a living condition. Due to rising costs and decreasing income, what was once their primary source of wealth, was slowly becoming an unlivable eyesore to the neighborhood. Habitat-MidOhio joined a number of affiliates around the country in beginning to do home repairs to address this new crisis.

Like many nonprofits starting a new program, we started very slowly and conservatively. There are so many things that have to be figured out when developing a new program. Program guidelines had to be created. Then we had to determine operational capacity and staffing. Once all of that was in place, we had to figure out how to fund the program, which often times can be the biggest challenge. Many funders want to see success before funding, so we have to invest a lot of money getting the program off the ground to prove impact, and then funders will want to fund the program.

Due to all of these factors, and many more, we were only able to complete about 20 home repairs in our first five years of the program. We had demonstrated definitively that helping to repair the homes of low income homeowners assisted them in staying in their homes, but we were never able to get it to scale. As we continued to see the need for repairs increasing in our community, we knew we needed to take bold steps to get to scale. We created a plan to sustainably grow the Home Repair program from serving an average of 4 families a year, to serving between 80 and 120 families a year, depending on need. Even more audacious was the timeline. We gave ourselves 2 years to get to that scale!

Our plan was built around an innovating funding model, so the biggest challenge to accomplishing this goal was identifying the families in need, and getting them through the application process to construction. As I started to look at this process, it quickly became clear that we needed to make significant improvements if we were going to get to scale. In the previous years, the vast majority of applications for home repair, nearly 94%, were being denied for various reasons. If our goal was to serve families, and more of them, then we needed to see why we were denying so many families.

As this was a project for my certification, I completed a full Define-Measure-Analyze-Improve-Control (DMAIC) approach. Although helpful given the scope of the project, there were a few steps and tools that really weren't all that necessary and could have been done without. Using the tools available to me, I began trying to determine the root cause to our problem. What I found was not surprising to those who were involved in the day-to-day operations. The biggest factor in us denying a request for repair was that they were outside of our determined service boundary limits. We found that in a two year period a full 45% of all requests were immediately denied due to location.

As a Habitat for Humanity affiliate, we have a specifically designated service area. Our service area encompasses 3 counties in Central Ohio surrounding Columbus. Given the size of area, we often choose to pick target areas for development. This ensures we have a much bigger impact on the community, and it allows us to maximize our resources, preventing a lot of wasted time traveling to various sites. When it comes to home construction, this model works great. So as we began our Home Repair program, we chose to keep the service boundaries of the program relatively near where we were also building new homes.

This decision worked well during the testing phase of the program, but as you can see, it was a large limiting factor. Unfortunately, it wasn't simply a decision to open up the service boundaries to match our affiliate's operating boundaries. It could impact staffing, fundraising, and other aspects of the program. After many conversations, it was determined that opening up our boundaries was the right step if our goal was to serve more families. That decision led to a significant increase in applications which we could review.

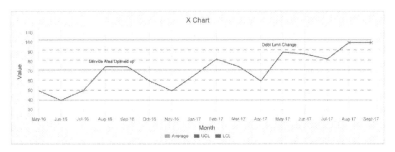

Figure 1. The percentage of applicants each month that were approved over a 16 month period. During this time we made 2 significant changes resulting in 2 clear shifts in the amount applications approved.

A second significant root cause of our denial rate was applicant debt, which resulted in a denial 18% of the time. As the Habitat Home Repair program involves an amount of payback that is based on income level, a family with too much debt would struggle with paying back a loan. In addition, certain federal laws limit how much debt we could allow a family to take out, which also hindered the ability of families to afford repairs. Upon further review of the data, we found those with the most debt tended to be the families who needed the most assistance with home repairs. Their debt payments prevented them from having the funds to put towards minor repairs, which when left alone, tended to escalate into major repairs.

The solution to that problem became clear as we looked at the data and met with families. If we could help families with repairs that tend to be less than $2500, we would be able to treat many of the problems which can be inexpensive to fix if caught right away, before they grow into much larger repairs. We structured the program to allow someone who had too much debt to still be able to receive services, just at a reduced amount, and with payment paid in full up front. This allowed families to get the services they need affordably without taking on the risk of more debt, or exceeding the debt limit. This opened the door to families who previously would have been denied immediately.

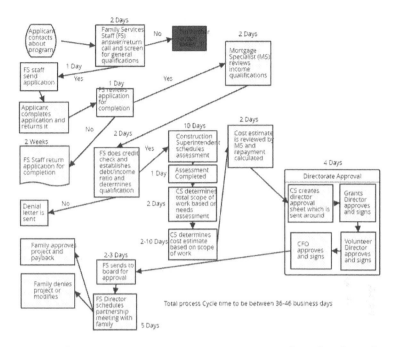

Figure 2. The pre-improvement process map was complicated and overly burdensome, with multiple unnecessary steps. The improved process had 6 unnecessary steps removed.

The final issue we identified in the process was the amount of waste in time and handling that was involved. We completed a process map and found a lot of time that was wasted with non-value add steps, including manual reviews and approvals of projects by multiple layers of directors and managers. In the early days of the program, we found that the average time from application to start of construction was nearly a year. One example of the waste was that once the project was approved for construction, it needed to be signed off by six Directors, including the Chief Financial Officer (CFO). Frequently, the project sign off sheet would go missing for days or weeks at a time, only to be found on the desk of one of the signers under a pile of other papers. When located, it usually took less than five minutes to review, sign off and be sent on down the line. All of that wasted time did nothing for the process, or the families. Upon reflection, there was a logical reason for the process to include this in the beginning, but it was completely unnecessary moving forward.

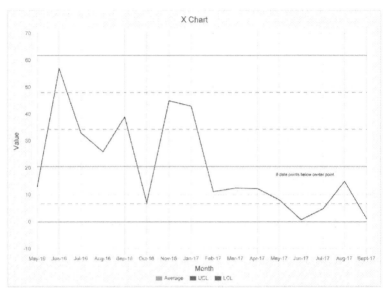

Figure 3. We saw a significant reduction in process days immediately after the process change. As noted though, with the process change we changed the bottleneck. We soon began approving more applicants than we could get through construction, which has now caused a much longer wait for construction.

Making these changes had immediate impact. We were able to see the number of approved applications jump to over 80%. This allowed us to have many more families which we could serve through this program. The year before we made these changes, we served a total of 8 families. This year we will exceed 80 families who received necessary home repairs, allowing them to stay affordably in their homes.

Of course with any change, as we made improvements in these steps of the process, we found the bottleneck moved somewhere else. We had originally thought that doing 80-120 repairs a year would meet demand, but we now believe that number is low. Initially, we were able to get families through the process, from application to completed construction, in just under 90 days. But as demand has picked up, we have built up quite a queue, now with the average time being over 180 days. We are now working to improve construction times in order to meet the demand we have that wasn't realized under the previous process.

Continuous Improvements

With the success of the improvements to our home repair program, we began to see opportunities throughout our organization for Lean Six Sigma principles to be used to manage change or improvements. To keep up the momentum, we needed to find a way to extend our capacity. As a nonprofit organization, we regularly get offers for volunteers and for internships. Most people who want to volunteer with us think about doing construction, so we rarely get to tap into the other skill sets they may have.

We were approached by a local university who had a large number of students in a Lean Six Sigma Green Belt class for undergraduates. These students needed projects to work on to help them complete their certification. This was a match made in heaven. Over the last few years, we have had 4 teams of students spend a semester working with us to solve some of the problems we have as an affiliate.

A majority of the projects we have them work on is within our ReStore program. Many Habitat for Humanity affiliates around the country operate a thrift store for building goods called ReStore, which sells gently used or new donated home goods to the public at a discount. The net funds help to fund our mission. Locally our two stores generate nearly $2 million in revenue each year, with a net profit of nearly $900,000. That money allows us to serve a significantly higher number of families each year.

Retail operations isn't a skill set most nonprofits have, so we have learned many lessons over the years on improving operations. But like any operation, there is plenty of opportunities for further progress. The outside teams we have come in bring a unique set of perspectives and expertise that we have found incredibly helpful.

The biggest driver of sales in our environment is getting donated product onto the sales floor as quickly and priced as accurately as possible. As a thrift store, customers generally come in a time or two a week to see what is new, and then move on. If a product is stuck in the donation process and not on the floor, we potentially miss out on a sale. Most of our product sells within 7 days of being donated, so even an extra few minutes or days in processing time can have a direct impact on sales.

The teams who have worked with us on solving this problem have taken the average throughput time of a donated item from greater than 180 minutes to less than 30 minutes. They have also created better visual standards, which have ensured more consistent pricing of goods, in order to maximize revenue. As each donated item may be unique, having consistent pricing guides and standards that are visual has made a huge impact on sales. It also has the added effect of limiting customer issues, as there is less obvious variability in the pricing of items.

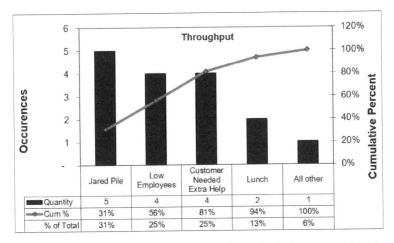

	Jared Pile	Low Employees	Customer Needed Extra Help	Lunch	All other
Quantity	5	4	4	2	1
Cum %	31%	56%	81%	94%	100%
% of Total	31%	25%	25%	13%	6%

Figure 4. The above Pareto Chart of defects shows the leading causes for why donations took more than 30 minutes to process and get on the sales floor. The "Jared Pile" represented items which did not have a standard pricing structure and required input from the manager. This created a bottleneck and caused the largest delays.

Another big impact these teams have had on our organization is the introduction of 5S workplace organization methods, which stands for Sort, Simplify, Sweep, Standardize and Sustain. Our donation processing areas can quickly become a mess of items, trash, and general chaos. After completing a 5S, the processing rooms have become much more streamlined, having removed bottlenecks and increased flow of goods. We also found the Standardize and Sustain steps were especially helpful to make long term change. We had often done a "cleanup" of the space, but formalizing the new state as the standard, and setting expectations of how frequently it would be reset to the standard has made the changes sustainable.

Figure 5 and 6. Our donation processing room after completion of a 5S. Room had been cleaned, unnecessary items removed, labels on where specific items go, and rearranged for better flow of material.

Figure 7 and 8. During a 5S, we noticed an obvious problem with our scrap metal station. It was disorganized and overflowing. It was moved and labeled with a visual cue of when it needs to be taken to the scrap yard. When it reaches the tape, it is time to remove it.

Lessons Learned

Here are a few lessons we have learned as we have begun using Lean Six Sigma principles within our organization.

- (1) *Often the problem is something we have created*

In our Home Repair program example, we were the ones who set the service boundaries for the program, we were the ones who demanded sign off on every project, and we were the ones who thought that too much debt should be an immediate disqualifier. All of these decisions were ones that we made. However, we ultimately changed our process when we took a stronger look at the goals of the program, the problem we were trying to solve, and a willingness to think beyond the bubble to see other solutions.

- (2) *The benefit of outside eyes in quickly identifying problems*

Having outside teams regularly work on projects has been very enlightening. They ask simple questions to understand the process that we are forced to answer, then we can quickly identify the source of issues, some of which we have fought with for years. When we do something for so long, we can become so desensitized to the steps that we can miss seeing what is quite obvious to those who are seeing something for the first time. We want to continue this process by using colleagues from other departments to be part of teams working on improvements, as their clear perspective is valuable in finding the root problem and identifying viable solutions.

- (3) *Empower employees as much as possible to improve the process and allow standards to be used to ensure quality*

All too often we have found a process that was put in place to ultimately create a bottleneck because we didn't empower staff to make the right decision. When we learned to trust staff, we improved quality, increased engagement and decreased waste in the process.

Moving forward, our goal is to create a culture of continuous improvement, where everyone feels empowered and encouraged to find solutions to problems on their own. When a solution cannot be easily identified and implemented, then creating a team and doing a formal project is justified. This "just do it" approach to process improvement will have longer lasting effects, and less time involved in making changes.

We have also been taking these lessons learned and sharing them around the Habitat for Humanity community. In March of 2019, I was able to lead a seminar with over 100 affiliate leaders from around the country on the basics of process improvement. This has led to the creation of an intracompany Yammer group, where we can share resources and discuss solutions to shared problems. Our hope would be to have process improvement and Lean Six Sigma become a regular skillset at many affiliates around the country.

Proceeds

Proceeds received from my chapter will be donated to Habitat for Humanity-MidOhio, which brings people together to inspire hope, build homes, empower families, and develop communities. Their vision is a world where everyone has a decent place to live. Learn more at https://www.habitatmidohio.org.

Founded in Americus, Georgia, USA, in 1976, Habitat for Humanity today operates around the globe and has helped build, renovate and repair close to 800,000 decent, affordable houses sheltering more than 3 million people worldwide.

Contact

In his role as Program Director, Philip Washburn is responsible for helping Habitat for Humanity-MidOhio reach its programmatic goals. His current focus is on improving program processes and outcomes in order to help the affiliate better serve more families. He is a Certified Black Belt in Lean Six Sigma which he has been successfully using to improve the organization's program, construction and ReStore processes. These improvements have allowed Habitat MidOhio to increase families served by 100% year over year with an expectation to quadruple growth over a 3 year period. Prior to joining Habitat, he has served in various management and director roles in the for-profit and nonprofit sectors.

Email: pwashburn@habitatmidohio.org

Resources and Next Steps

Helping nonprofits

Would you like to volunteer your experience with a not-for-profit organization? You can search for volunteers groups near you (both US and International), and get advice on setting up your own volunteer group at the following website: http://www.leansixsigmaforgood.com/local-lean-six-sigma-and-nonprofit-groups/

Volunteer from Lean Portland help map the donation receiving floor layout at the Gresham (OR) ReStore.

Sharing your experiences

If you know someone who has spent time helping nonprofits or not-for-profit organizations apply process improvement techniques, please contact me at brion@biz-pi.com for more information about contributing to Volume 2.

Learn more

If you'd like to search for more case studies and examples of Lean and Six Sigma applied to nonprofits in different countries and different types of organizations, or to connect with our social media and networking platforms, please visit http://LeanSixSigmaforGood. com.

Made in the USA
Columbia, SC
21 February 2023

12728710R00086